HORRIBLE HISTORIES

SCOTLAND

Terry Deary Illustrated by **Martin Brown**

SCHOLASTIC

This book is for the librarians, pupils and staff at
Buckie High School, Scotland

Scholastic Children's Books,
Euston House, 24 Eversholt Street,
London NW1 1DB, UK

A division of Scholastic Ltd
London ~ New York ~ Toronto ~ Sydney ~ Auckland
Mexico City ~ New Delhi ~ Hong Kong

First published in the UK as Bloody Scotland by Scholastic Ltd, 1998
This edition published 2017

ISBN 978 1407 18569 9

Page layout services provided by Quadrum Solutions Ltd, Mumbai, India
Printed and bound in the UK by CPI Group (UK) Ltd, Croydon, CR0 4YY

4 6 8 10 9 7 5 3

www.scholastic.co.uk

CONTENTS

Introduction

History can be horrible. But it can be horribler in some places than in others.

Take Scotland. A small country, where life could be hard, and where the people learned to be tough. But it was next to a bigger country, where life and the people could be softer – and unfortunately there were more of them.

It's a bit like little David living next door to Goliath. Every now and then David brings the giant crashing down – but when Goliath gets his revenge then he can turn very nasty indeed...

The trouble is the history books are written by the 'winners'. So English history books can tell all sorts of lies about the Scots!

1. Battle. Result: Scotland 1 – England 0
2. Soccer. Result: England 2 – Scotland 0

When the English did horrible things to the Scots, the English historians told whacking great fibs to make it sound as if the Scots deserved it. For example, when the English executed the Scottish leader William Wallace, they killed him very slowly and painfully. A monk called William Rishanger was an historian who wrote...

Wallace's men carried babies on the end of their spears, burned children alive in their schools and murdered people as they prayed in their churches

Rubbish! When Wallace was supposed to be doing this in St Albans, he was in fact 300 miles away on the Scottish Borders. William Rishanger was telling whacking great fibs.

And the English tell lies about Scots being mean. You know the sort of thing...

HAMISH McNASTY FOUND A PAIR OF CRUTCHES AND HE BROKE BOTH HIS LEGS SO HE COULD USE THEM. EVERY TIME HE TAKES 10ᴾ OUT OF HIS SPORRAN THE QUEEN BLINKS IN THE LIGHT. HE EVEN KEEPS HIS WRIST WATCH IN THE BANK 'COS HE'S TRYING TO SAVE TIME. THEY SAY HAMISH GOES TO A WEDDING WITH ELASTIC ON HIS CONFETTI BECAUSE HE'S SO MEAN

Of course, there are some true stories about the Scots which show they had to be 'careful' with their money. Some Scots were so poor that they couldn't afford a coffin for their dead family. It would have been shameful to carry them to their grave wrapped up in a sheet, so they hired a 'common coffin'. The corpse was popped into this special coffin and carried to the grave. The bottom was on a hinge, which was opened to let the body fall into the grave. The coffin could be used again. Very sensible.

The English make heartless remarks because the Scots enjoy bagpipes that sound like tortured cats. You won't find rotten jokes like that in this book (well, maybe one). But you *will* find true stories about men like James Reid. His crime was to be caught with a set of bagpipes and put on trial. A judge at York said they were an 'instrument of war'. James Reid was found guilty and hanged. (He probably gave up playing the bagpipes after he was hanged.)

The English make fun of Scottish poets who write about haggis puddings. There's nothing wrong with writing a poem to a pudding. There is plenty wrong with *bad* poetry, so this book will make fun of that instead. Even the Scots have to laugh at lines like...

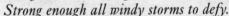

> *Beautiful new railway bridge of the silvery Tay,*
> *With your strong brick piers and buttresses in grand*
>   *array,*
> *And your 13 central girders, which seem to my eye*
> *Strong enough all windy storms to defy.*

WELL IF I
DON'T LAUGH
I'M GOING
TO CRY

And that's not just horrible poetry ... it's horrible history too because the bridge blew away and killed 90 people.

There is no limit to the cruelty that the English bullies have inflicted on the poor Scots. But, now, the biggest insult of all! The evil English have produced a Horrible History of Scotland ... and it's written by an Englishman! This disgraceful book should be banned. (So read it quickly and buy ten copies for your friends before it is!)

Take your Pict – Dark Age Scotland

Your teacher won't know this, but a Scotsman invented prehistoric monsters! No, he wasn't God. He was the Scottish archaeologist Daniel Wilson who invented the word 'prehistoric' to mean 'a time before written history'. If it wasn't for Dan we'd still be saying things like 'monsters-from-the-time-before-written-history'.

Early historic Scotland followed prehistoric Scotland, surprisingly enough. It's called the Dark Ages because we don't know a lot about it – we're in the dark, in fact. That's a pity, because it must have been an exciting place to live … and an easy place to die.

Timeline – Dark Age deeds

AD 80 The Roman governor of Britain, Julius Agricola, invades Scotland – he calls the place 'Caledonia' and goes on to massacre up to 10,000 Caledonians.

122 Emperor Hadrian orders a wall to be built from the Tyne to the Solway to keep the Picts out of Roman England.

140 Romans build another wall, made of turf and timber, further north from the Firth to the Clyde – but it's a struggle to keep the Picts out (or *in*). This is known as the Antonine Wall.

211 The Romans finally give up trying to conquer the Picts and go back to having Hadrian's Wall as their border.

296 Picts, Scots and Saxons attack Roman London. Maybe they wanted to play a football international?

409 The Romans leave and the Scots tribes (from Ireland) move in to south-west Pictland and found the kingdom of Dalriada.

563 St Columba, from Ireland, starts converting the Picts and Scots to the Christian religion. He sets up a monastery on Iona.

617 St Donan, a missionary, is killed along with 52 followers on the island of Eigg in a row with Pict warriors about some sheep.

672 Ecgfrith of Northumbria massacres a Pict army and a lot of its leaders. But he'll pay for it.

685 Ecgfrith tries to invade Pictland to teach the Pict raiders a lesson. Picts massacre him and his army at Nechtan Pass. Some lesson.

730 The king of the Picts defeats the Scots but...

806 Vikings arrive and mince monks on Iona.

844 The Scot king, Kenneth MacAlpine, fights the Vikings and takes back the Scot lands plus the Pict lands. He is now king of the Kingdom of Alban.

1018 In the battle of Carham the northern English are defeated and the winner, King Malcolm II, becomes king of a land known as Scotland.

Painted people

In 1603 James VI of Scotland wanted to prove that he was the rightful king. He *said* that his family could be traced all the way back to Noah and the flood when the animals went in two by two. (If you believe this then your brain cell will not go *anywhere* two by two because you probably only have one.)

The truth is that the Picts probably arrived in Scotland about 500 BC. They may have been Celtic tribes, like the Welsh and the Irish. The land was probably empty apart from a few prehistoric cave people around the coasts. (Those prehistoric Scots are often called 'the beaker people' – because their bodies have been found buried with beakers, *not* because they had beaks.)

The early Picts may have called themselves Cruithne – 'wheat-growers' – but the Romans came along and changed all that. They called them the 'Picts' and the name stuck like cold porridge on the roof of your mouth.

Now 'Pict' could come from the Roman word for 'painter' or 'painted'. This gives clever historians the chance to argue *why* the Romans gave them this name…

Many Scots today still remember being taught that the tribes were called Picts because they painted themselves blue instead of wearing clothes! That's nonsense – anyone without clothes in the Highlands would *turn* blue with the cold – they wouldn't *have* to paint themselves!

What's the truth? Take your Pict!

Wotsa Scot?

If you think the name 'Pict' is peculiar then the 'Scot' name is even more weird.

Just before the year AD 500, Fergus MacErc and his five brothers arrived from Ireland. They took over a Pict area and called their kingdom Dalriada – after their homeland in Ireland.

Everyone north of the English border *should* be called 'Ercs', but Fergus and his tribe called themselves 'Scots'. Why?

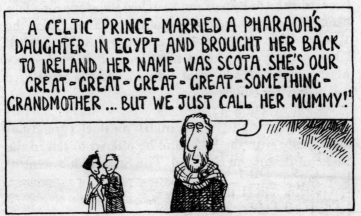

A CELTIC PRINCE MARRIED A PHARAOH'S DAUGHTER IN EGYPT AND BROUGHT HER BACK TO IRELAND. HER NAME WAS SCOTA. SHE'S OUR GREAT-GREAT-GREAT-GREAT-SOMETHING-GRANDMOTHER ... BUT WE JUST CALL HER MUMMY!"

In the Bible there's a story of Jacob falling asleep with his head on a pillow of stone. Scota brought this stone with her from Egypt and Fergus took it across to Pictland. It's known as the 'stone of destiny' and this stone caused a lot of trouble over the next 1,500 years. The English pinched it and used it as a coronation stone for centuries until 1997, when it was returned to Scotland.

(To be *really* fair the Scots should now send it back to Egypt so Jacob can get a decent night's sleep. Bet they don't.)

Did you know…?
The Scots believed that all their kings should be crowned while sitting on Fergus MacErc's 'stone of destiny'. In 1297 King Edward I of England decided to put a stop to this nonsense. He pinched the stone from the throne at

1. Of course some historians just *have* to disagree. They say 'Scot' comes from the Latin word for 'pirates'.

Scone and carried it back to England. English kings were crowned on it in London. It stayed in England for 700 years.

Or *did* it?

There's a story that the monks of the abbey at Scone knew what he was up to and switched the stone for a fake before Edward got there. The real stone was carried to the Western Isles where it has remained to this day. English kings weren't crowned on the 'stone of destiny'. They were crowned on a lump of old rock and the Scots have had a 700-year laugh.

Nice story, but is it true?

Here's a clue. In 1328, Edward III (the thief's grandson) made peace with the Scots and he offered to return the 'stone of destiny' to Scotland. The Scots didn't want it! Why not?

Maybe because they knew it was a fake.

Roman in the gloamin'

The popular Scots singer Harry Lauder wrote the song...

*Roamin' in the gloamin' by the bonnie
    banks of Clyde,
Roamin' in the gloamin' with a lassie
    by my side.
When the sun has gone to rest,
That's the time that I like best.*

This song is about roaming in the gloaming – or the evening. But 2,000 years before Harry wrote his song there were *Romans* in the Scottish gloamin' who did *not* enjoy it one little bit. Some historians reckon up to 50,000 Romans died trying to bring peace to Pictland (or calm to Caledonia).

But don't feel too sorry for the Romans. Remember – *they* started it! The *Romans* were the invaders.

YOU'VE PICT THE WRONG PEOPLE TO INVADE, JIMMY!

The Romans didn't conquer Pictland. But they did bring all the Pict tribes together. They forgot their squabbles amongst each other to face the rotten Romans.

At the battle of Mons Graupius in AD 84 the Picts lost. The Romans burned Pict homes and drove the surviving warriors into the mountains.

That's when the Pict leader Calgacus made one of those famous speeches that has gone down in history...

The Romans make a desert and they call it peace.

Great stuff. Pity that line was probably just made up by a Roman writer called Tacitus... But learn the line anyway and get better marks in your history test. Some historians say Tacitus even made up the Pict leader Calgacus!

Then suddenly, two years after winning at Mons Graupius, the Romans packed up and left the Picts in peace. (There was trouble over in Romania and they couldn't spare the troops to stay in Scotland.)

Another 40 years later, Emperor Hadrian built his wall and said, 'Right lads, the Roman Empire stops *here*. Let the Picts have their rotten Caledonia.' (Except Hadrian said it in Latin.)

Gore for the gods

Historians know a lot about the ancient gods of the rest of Britain, but not a lot about the gods that the Picts worshipped. Archaeologists have dug up some clues, though. Here's how to worship your old gods...

Stone circles

The English have one great stone circle called Stonehenge, but the Scots have *thousands* of stone circles and standing stones. Some have pictures on them – animals, birds and fish are popular signs – but most are plain.

Stone footprints have also been found carved into the rock. Why? Who knows? Historians guess it was to do with crowning a new king.

If you have a spare five years you could build a stone circle in your back garden. (If you just have a spare five minutes you could use cardboard boxes instead.)

The Picts would be sun-worshippers like the other Celts. Once you have your circle you need to do some worshipping.

Again we have to work from clues that archaeologists have dug up...

Sacrifices

The gods get hungry, the same as everybody else. Of course they can't be expected to harvest crops or raise animals. Humans do that. So, if *you* give some of your food to the gods then *they'll* make sure you have a good harvest next year.

First, dig a pit. Then kill an animal (a cow, a sheep, a goat, a pig or a teacher), and roast it. (If you haven't got a dead animal then you could try offering a beefburger or a fish finger.)

Have a good feast with your friends, but don't forget to drop some of the food in the pit for the gods. They'll probably like the bits that you don't like, so that's all right.

IS HADRIAN'S WALL FINISHED?

OCH NO, IT'S STILL MORE LIKE HADRIAN'S FENCE

DO YOU THINK STANDING STONES EVER WANT TO SIT DOWN?

Customs

And if you *really* want to make the gods happy then capture a king and drown him in a well. This Pict custom brought luck – but it ruined your drinking water.

And, when you choose a new king, you must ride off and steal cattle from the tribe next door to celebrate. (If they try to stop you, drown their king.)

The Monk Gildas summed up these Pict people around AD 600…

17

> The Picts and Scots are wandering thieves who have no taste for war. They are allies because they share their greed for bloodshed

Not a very nice thing to say about the ancient Scots. But some English writers are still saying that sort of thing about their neighbours over the border!

Did you know…?
Old King Cole was a merry old soul … until he went to Scotland? King Cole of ancient Britain was killed by the Scottish chieftain, Fergus.

Signs of the times

The Pict pictures on stones are famous. But they did have a curious form of writing too. There are not many of these signs scratched on to stones but there are enough for us to understand them.

This alphabet is known as 'ogham'.

The writer draws a straight line then makes marks to the right or left of the line. Here's the ogham alphabet…

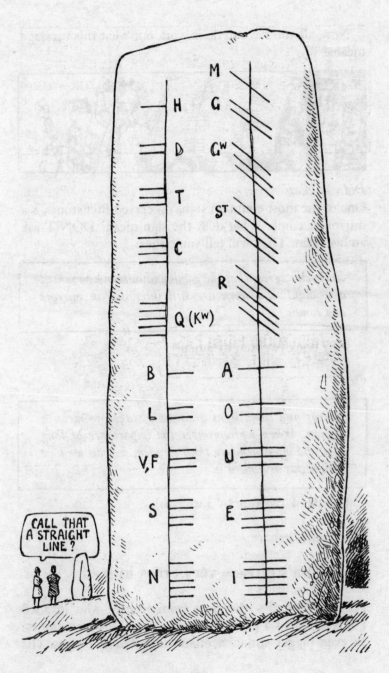

Now, all you have to do is work out what this message means!

Did you know…?
One of the most common signs on carved Pict stones is a mirror or comb. What does the sign mean? DON'T ask an historian. They will tell you either…

> *Everyone agrees that the comb and mirror sign means a woman … women are still interested in mirrors and combs.*

1987 book (written by a man)

Or…

> *Mirror and comb signs are usually taken to mean a woman. When we remember the importance of long hair and moustaches to the Pict men, we can see how foolish this argument is.*

1996 book (written by a woman)

Take your Pict!

Columba's cross – very cross indeed

Fergus MacErc – the Scot from Ireland who invaded Pictland – had a great-grand-nephew. This man caused an even bigger stir in Scotland than Uncle Fergus. His name was Columba. A bad-tempered Irish prince in the MacErc family.

In AD 563 he was more or less told, 'Get on your horse and get out of town … or Ireland, at any rate.'

So he crossed the Irish Sea and settled on the island of Iona. Unlike Great-grand-uncle he didn't bring a dirty great lump of stone. He brought a new religion. Christianity.

Clever Columba *didn't* upset the Picts by knocking down their stone circles. Instead he built his churches inside the circles.

Did you know…?
The Scots word for church is 'kirk'. And the word 'kirk' is said to come from 'circle'. Kirk-kirkle-circle, geddit?

You can read about Columba converting the Picts to Christianity in boring books. This is a *horrible* history, so here are some of the more terrible tales…

And, of course, Columba was the first person to meet the famous Loch Ness monster. He defeated it, naturally. (Sadly he didn't have a camera phone with him because they hadn't been invented yet. If he had then he could have made a fortune from selling the video.)

Some legends record that the monk died in Nessie's jaws and Columba brought him back to life.

In 597 Columba failed to bring himself back to life.

Then there was Ken

After Columba the history of Scotland is a bit uncertain. The Picts and Scots lived side by side (and probably fought side by side against the English of Northumbria). Then the Viking invaders arrived from Norway and Denmark.

A strange thing seems to have happened. The Pict kings were killed off by the Vikings, and their Scot neighbour, Kenneth MacAlpine, took advantage of the Pict problems.

Ken was crafty. His men were facing defeat at the hands of the Picts...

Not only did the Picts make him their king, but they also let him change their name to 'Scots'.

No one can explain why the Picts let Kenneth MacAlpine take over as their ruler, but he was the first king of a country we can now call Scotland.

Monarchs and mayhem

Scotland and its kings (and queens) have a horrible history of their own. If there was a world record for murdered kings then Scotland would probably be its proud holder.

And if there was another record for kings who were

murderers then Scotland would probably hold that, too. In the 200 years after Kenneth MacAlpine's death there were dozens of kings who each ruled for two or three years then died dreadfully.

There is not much written history for this period ... kings didn't hang around long enough to write stories of 'My life and times' (or, in the case of King Gryme, 'My life and Grymes').

There are stories from this age, but they're as easy to believe as 'Cinderella meets Red Riding Hood and they eat the three little pigs'. Still, they're good and gory stories. So, find some snotty little child, sit them on your knee and say, 'I'm going to tell you a story! Are you sitting comfortably? Then I'll begin. This is the story of King Kenneth II who ruled from AD 971 to 995 and Queen Finella.' Both are real historical characters, but can you believe the story of Ken's end...?

Killing King Ken II

Once upon a time there was a beautiful queen and her name was Queen Finella.

Finella was lovely, but she was ever so sad because her dear son Malcolm had died. She cried and cried, but that did no good. So, in the end, she decided to find out how Malcolm had died. They say she was a little bit of a witch, but a good witch.

Finella went to her cauldron and stirred the magic brew, chanting...

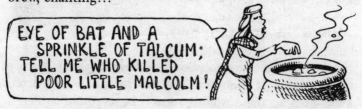

EYE OF BAT AND A SPRINKLE OF TALCUM; TELL ME WHO KILLED POOR LITTLE MALCOLM!

The pot bubbled and boiled and then it answered...

YOUR MALCOLM DIED, THE POOR YOUNG THING,
MURDERED BY A ROTTEN KING!
DRY YOUR EYES, GOOD SWEET FINELLA
OLD KING KEN'S THE GUILTY FELLA

Now the only King Ken that Queen Fin kenned (knew), was cruel King Kenneth in Kincardine, the kingdom next door.

Finella knew she wasn't strong enough to raise an army and go to war with King Kenneth. So she came up with a clever plan instead.

She used all her magic arts to make a brass statue of King Kenneth. It was as yellow as Finella's curls and as shiny as the sun on the loch. In the glistening statue's hand was an apple covered in a rainbow of jewels. When the statue was finished, she put it in the middle of her finest room in Fettercairn and invited King Kenneth to come and see it.

Kenneth arrived and Finella gave a low curtsey. 'I am your humble servant, King Ken,' she said. 'Please accept this gift.'

Cruel Ken looked at the statue and said, 'I'll never get that thing home on horseback!'

Finella smiled sweetly and said, 'Just the apple, Ken. Reach out and take the apple.'

The killing king stretched out a hand while Finella ducked. As soon as his hand touched the apple a dozen hidden crossbows in the walls fired poison arrows into his body.

'It was all a trick!' Ken cried as he died.

'And it jolly well serves you right,' Finella said with her sweet smile.

And Queen Finella lived happily ever after until she died an even more horrible death than Kenneth.

The end.

Miserable Macbeth

Scotland has one king who is famous round the world for his homicidal horrors. He ruled from 1040 till 1057 and is famous because William Shakespeare wrote a play about him 550 years later. Ask your teacher, 'Which Scottish king did Shakespeare write a play about?'

The teacher will say, 'Macbeth.'

You will say, 'Will you tell me about it?'

And the teacher will explain...

- Macbeth invited King Duncan to his palace.
- He waited till Duncan fell asleep.
- He crept into Duncan's bedroom and stabbed the old man to death.

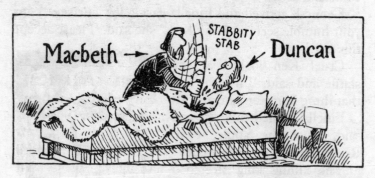

Then you can say, 'What happened to Macbeth in the end?'

Teacher will say, 'His enemies attacked him at Dunsinane and cut off his head.'

Then you can say, 'That's shocking!'

Teacher will say, 'Macbeth was a cruel man. He deserved it.'

And you can say, 'No! I don't mean *Macbeth's* story is shocking. I mean your Scottish *history* is shocking!' Then you explain...

- Duncan wasn't an old man. He was 27 years old and younger than Macbeth.
- Duncan didn't go to Macbeth's castle as a guest. They met in battle.
- Macbeth killed Duncan in the battle, not by stabbing him in his sleep.
- And Macbeth didn't die at Dunsinane. He lost the battle of Dunsinane but didn't die for another three years.

Then walk away with a sad shake of the head.

> *HORRIBLE HISTORIES* HEALTH WARNING: If you have a grumpy teacher who can't take a joke, then *don't* walk away. Wear your best trainers and *run!*

Of course this muddled Scottish history is all Will Shakespeare's fault. But he was an Englishman, so what do you expect? It is no use trying this quiz on a Scottish history teacher, of course.

Funny food, cwaint customs and sporran sports

Scottish scran

If you want to understand a Scot, you have to understand what he or she eats … and drinks, of course.

The Scots are proud of their food and drink, but do they always tell the truth about its origins? Who is being honest here?

So who's telling the truth? Sadly, Britannia probably has her facts right – though you'll always find some Scottish professor ready to argue.

Haggis was popular in England until the end of the 1700s. It was the poet Robbie Burns who made it Scotland's national dish when he wrote his poem about it.

BUT WE *DID* INVENT KIPPERS AND MARMALADE AND WHISKY

I SUPPOSE THAT'S TRUE

Kippers – smoked herring – were produced in the village of Finnan (near Aberdeen). And the herring found that smoking was bad for their health.

Horrible haggis
It doesn't matter who invented it, Scotland is now famous for the 'haggis'.

Robbie Burns's poem 'To a haggis', calls it the 'great chieftain o' the puddin' race'. Here's a quick guide, in case you fancy chomping on the chieftain...

1 First kill your sheep. (If you haven't any beef suet handy then you may have to kill a cow as well.)

BAA

2 Cut out the sheep's heart, its liver, its lungs and its stomach. Turn the stomach inside out to clean out all that half-chewed grass (not to mention the crunched beetles that were living on the grass and the sheep-droppings that the sheep accidentally sucked up).

3 Meanwhile pop the heart, liver and lungs into some boiling, salted water. (If you get bored waiting for them to cook, then take the sheep's wool and knit yourself a kilt.)

4 When it's all nicely cooked then mince it all together. (I hope you remembered to wash your hands.)

5 Stir in salt, pepper, nutmeg, cayenne and a chopped onion. Then add a pound of chopped beef suet, oatmeal and a cup of gravy. Mix it all together. (Keep stirring till it looks like a hedgehog after the 15th lorry has run over it.)

6 Stuff the sheep's stomach with the mixture. (Remember to stitch up one end before you start packing it in the other end – otherwise there'll be a mess on the floor.)

7 Boil the pudding in a large pan of water for three hours. (You'll be getting hungry by now. That's all right – you'll enjoy the haggis all the more when you get to eat it, so keep your hands off that bag of crisps.)

8 Invite your favourite teacher to dinner. (Or, even better, the teacher who gave you the worst report in the universe.)

9 Serve the haggis on a well-starched napkin. (A handkerchief that you've just blown your nose on will not do.)

10 Watch your guest eat the haggis with chappit tatties and bashed neeps (that's mashed potato and mashed swede to you ignorant readers) – and, while they're eating, tell them what's inside!

If your guest is religious then you may like to recite a couple of lines of Robbie Burns's 'Selkirk Grace' before they tuck in. Burns said some people have food but can't eat it, other people need food but can't get any. He ends…

> *But we hae¹ meat and we can eat,*
> *And so the Lord be thankit.*

1. 'Hae' is Scots for 'have'. Until you learn to speak Scots in a later chapter you'll just have to suffer these interruptions.

Peculiar porridge

Porridge has been a popular breakfast in Scotland for hundreds of years. But it's not just *eating* porridge that will help you understand the Scots. It's the *way* they eat it. Believe it or not there's more than one way to eat a plate of porridge! Here are just three…

South Uist porridge

Porridge is served in a soup plate on your right. Cold milk is served in a bowl in front of you. Use a large spoon and take a little of the hot porridge. Dip the spoon of porridge into the milk and place the milk and porridge into the mouth. Try not to drop the porridge off the spoon into the bowl of milk!

Aberdeen porridge

Serve the porridge in a large plate. Pour cold milk on top of it so the porridge is like an island. Scoop up a little milk and a little porridge on the spoon and eat it. Do  not mix it all up. Only an English eater would do that.

St Kilda porridge

It's said that the islanders of St Kilda enjoyed porridge for breakfast with a puffin added for extra flavour. Yes, that cute little bird with the rainbow beak.

That beak must have been a bit crunchy and the feet would be too chewy. I guess they must have just added the *meat* of the puffins. (Somebody should sell this idea to the supermarkets. The puffin meat could be sweetened for children and sold as a breakfast cereal. They could call it 'sugar puffins'!)

Tatties and herring

The English have fish and chips. The Scots have fish and boiled potatoes.

When Scots started to get a taste for English food like beef and beer in the 1880s, there was a protest song written about it...

*Now your hard-working Scotsman's gone crazy, I fear,
Every day he must have a bit beef and some beer.
But you do not know, and you're maybe not caring,
Your natural food, it is tatties and herring.
Tatties and herring, tatties and herring,
Your natural food, it is tatties and herring.*

(Make up your own tune and entertain the school dinner ladies with that one!)

The English say fish and chips taste best when eaten with the fingers – and that's what the Scots say about their 'tatties and herring'.

The potatoes are boiled in the same pot as the fish, then served on a plate. Take a potato in your left hand and take a pinch of the herring in your right. Eat one after the other. 'Left-right, left-right, left-right, ouch!' (The ouch is when you bite your finger by mistake, which serves you right for not using a knife and fork.)

Tasty tips for Scottish scran

Scottish cookbooks have some delightful hints on improving your food. Here are some you may care to mention to your parents as they prepare your tea...

1 Wind-blown fish Haddock tastes better if it's been hung up in a draughty passage for a day to dry. Just inside the front door may be nice.

> When you've skinned the fish you should take out its eyes and pass a string through the eye sockets so the fish can be hung up.

2 Nettle kail Forget the pancakes. On Shrove Tuesday you should be eating soup made from a one-year-old cockerel and a bunch of fresh nettles. The poet, Thomas Campbell, said...

> *In Scotland I have slept in nettle sheets and dined off a nettle tablecloth. The stalks of old nettles can be beaten into a yarn and woven into cloth. I have heard my mother say that she thinks nettle cloth is tougher than linen.*

Fine, Thomas, but you wouldn't catch me sleeping in a bed of nettles!

3 Broth This soup was always an important food for rich and poor in Scotland. Lumps of beef and chopped bones were boiled with herbs...

> a) Add marigold petals for colour.
> b) Skim off the grease and let it set at the back door. This is called 'dripping' and should be kept for beggars.

> c) Drop some large hens into the pot so they can be boiling while the soup is stewing. Take them out and serve the hens separately for dinner.
> d) Keep a lid on the pot so soot doesn't drop in.

Sensible tip, that last one; after all, you don't want soot and sour chicken, do you?

4 Powsodie This is a soup made with a sheep's head split in half by the butcher. The brains are taken out to be eaten separately.

> Take the head to the local blacksmith. He will hold it over his forge to singe off all the wool before the head is put in the cooking pot.

Extra tip: give the eyes to your head teacher because schools get extra money if they have more pupils.

Did you know...?

Many poor Highlanders survived on tatties and herring – around Inverness the labourers would eat an average of four kilos a day. (Weigh four kilos of potatoes and see if you could eat that every day!) They suffered terribly when their potatoes were struck by disease in 1836.

Scottish food you may like to try

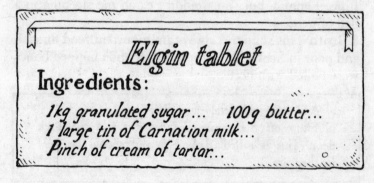

Elgin tablet

Ingredients:

1kg granulated sugar...   100g butter...
1 large tin of Carnation milk...
Pinch of cream of tartar...

Equipment:

Large saucepan
2 swiss roll tins

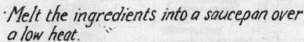

Method:

- *Melt the ingredients into a saucepan over a low heat.*
- *Bring to the boil and boil hard for 15 minutes.*
- *Grease the swiss roll tins.*
- *Pour the mixture into the tins and leave to set.*
- *Cut it into squares before it is completely cool.*
- *You have something like fudge or caramel.*
- *Eat it.*

Note: This 'tablet' is not something you eat when you're sick. It's something so delicious you will probably eat it *until* you are sick!

Quick quiz: What 'impossible' Scottish food is popular around the world?
a) Edinburgh rock made from Glasgow rocks
b) Vegetarian haggis
c) Bagpipe-flavoured dog food

Answer: **b** Haggis is a sheep's insides stuffed into a sheep's stomach. Yet a haggis manufacturer is producing a 'vegetarian haggis' made with nuts and mushrooms stuffed inside goodness-knows-what. But if it's 'vegetarian' it has no sheep bits in at all, so it can't be a 'haggis'. Of every eight haggis sold, one is 'vegetarian'. Very odd.

Deadly drink

Scotland's most famous drink is its whisky, of course. It's so important that in 1695 rum was banned in Scotland because it was bad for the whisky business. The lawmakers said rum was a drug that was bad for your health. The truth was...

GOVERNMENT WARNING
DRINKING RUM IS BAD
FOR YOUR WEALTH

Of course whisky could be just as deadly as rum. Doctors in the 1700s needed dead bodies for examination and dissection. To keep them fresh the bodies were preserved in cheap whisky. If it will pickle a body imagine what it must do to a drinker's gut!

Scottish drinkers probably needed something warming like whisky. In 1200 the historian Hector Boece said that Scotland was so cold the beer froze and was sold in lumps by the pound!

Cwaint customs

Another way to try and understand people is through their customs. The Scots have always had their own customs and some of them may seem very strange to us today.

You have to get the customs right, of course, otherwise you may have the wrong effect. Pair these partners and get it right ... or else!

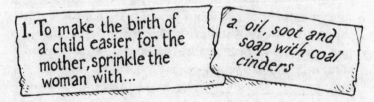

1. To make the birth of a child easier for the mother, sprinkle the woman with...

a. oil, soot and soap with coal cinders

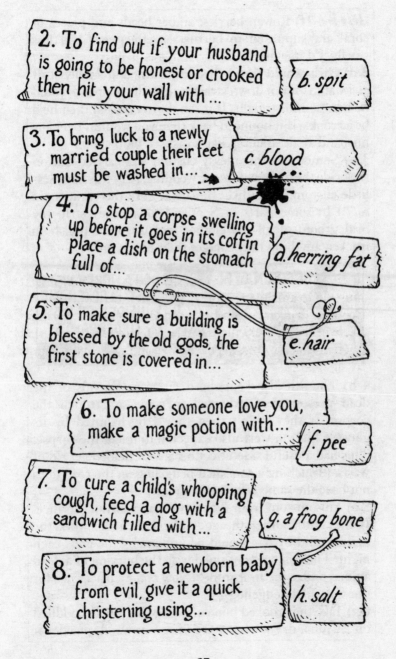

2. To find out if your husband is going to be honest or crooked then hit your wall with ...

b. spit

3. To bring luck to a newly married couple their feet must be washed in....

c. blood

4. To stop a corpse swelling up before it goes in its coffin place a dish on the stomach full of...

d. herring fat

5. To make sure a building is blessed by the old gods, the first stone is covered in...

e. hair

6. To make someone love you, make a magic potion with...

f. pee

7. To cure a child's whooping cough, feed a dog with a sandwich filled with...

g. a frog bone

8. To protect a newborn baby from evil, give it a quick christening using...

h. salt

37

Answers: **1f)** Rowan berries, amber beads and pieces of coral are supposed to be just as effective. (And less smelly, I'd imagine.)

2 d) Girls would throw this disgusting and smelly stuff at a wall. If it ran down straight then the husband would be honest and straight. If it ran down crooked then he'd be a crook. (If it bounced back then you wouldn't get any husband at all smelling like a disused chip shop.)

3 a) Sometimes this messy custom was carried out on the bride the night before the wedding. (Try this harmless little custom if you like. But make sure the cinders are *cold*!) In some parts of Scotland today, they strip the bridegroom of all his clothes and use boot polish to blacken anything they can get their hands on!

4 h) The salt also kept the devil away. Friends of the dead person were expected to come and touch the corpse. If they didn't then they'd be haunted by its ghost. Children were also expected to touch the corpse. This had a useful side-effect because it helped get rid of warts. (Touching a squashed hedgehog on the road does not have the same effect, I'm afraid.)

5 c) This custom from Pict times was a sort of sacrifice. If they didn't offer the gods blood then the work the builders did by day would be undone by the gods each night. The custom continued with the burying of a dead animal under the first stone. (Now *that's* a better use for the squashed hedgehog!)

6 g) Take the crooked bone of a frog that has been killed on 24 June, dry it over a fire of rowan wood, powder it and sprinkle it over the food of the one you love. (If the one you love is a vegetarian then you'd better not tell them what you've done! They may tell you to hop it; or the shock could make them croak!)

I DIDN'T HAVE THE HEART TO KILL IT!

7 e) Cut the child's hair and feed it to the dog between two slices of bread. If the dog coughed then the child was cured. (Because the dog had probably caught the cough, you understand. Make sure you give this to the nasty mutt down the street; the one that chases your poor little Tiddles.)

8b) Babies could die before they got a church christening so the midwife would use water to bless it. But spit has magical, good-luck properties. Parents in Britain *still* believe this – though they don't always know it! The healing power of spit is where you get the idea of 'kiss it better'. (That's probably why footballers run around spitting so much!)

Sporran sports

Some of the most curious Scottish customs of all are sporting ones.

In the 1500s Mary Queen of Scots enjoyed golf and billiards and was a great shot. (When she tried to pot the English throne Elizabeth I sent her to the back of the cue.) After her beheading, Mary Queen of Scots's lips were seen to move. (Maybe, as her head hit the basket, she was trying to cry, 'Hole in one!')

Scotland has its own national sports. For example there is a sort of bowls played with flat stones scooted over frozen ponds. It's called 'curling'. (No, it is *not* the national sport of Scottish hairdressers.)

Here are some other peculiar pastimes the Scots have tried through the ages...

Hurley hacket (or summer sledging)

To play
1 Take a dead horse (plenty of those around in the Middle Ages) and boil its head till the flesh drops off.
2 Take the clean skull to Heading Hill in Stirling. (It's really Be-heading Hill because that was the place where they gave chops to tops.)
3 Use the skull as a sledge and slide down the hill.
If you can't get to Stirling then try Calton Hill in Edinburgh, where young people also enjoyed this sport.

If you haven't got a dead horse (or 'hack') then you can't play hurley hacket. But you can play hurley haaky if you have a haaky – a cow.

> *HORRIBLE HISTORIES* HEALTH WARNING: If you really must try this sport, mind the cow's teeth don't bite you, especially if it died of mad cow disease.

Did you know...?
The champion at hurley hacket was King James V, who preferred this sort of sledging to ruling the country.

Highland Games
Scotland is famous for its Highland Games. But the first Highland Games to be held in North America were between Scottish soldiers and Creek Indians. (Did they play tossing the tepee?) In the USA there are now over a hundred Highland Games held every year. (Hopefully they are sponsored by good Scottish Americans like McDonalds!)

Twisting the cow

At the Invergarry Games of 1820 the events included 'dancing, piping, lifting a heavy stone, throwing the hammer and running from the island to Invergarry and back' (six miles). But the strangest event was 'Twisting the legs off a cow'.

You need
Dead cows – one for each competitor.

To play
1 Twist off all four legs of the cow.
2 The person who does it in the shortest time is the winner.

The prize
One fat sheep.
At Invergarry at least one man succeeded and won the sheep, but it took him about an hour.

One of the most famous Scottish games is...

Tossing the caber

You need
A caber – that's a tree trunk without its branches. (Use a telegraph pole if you haven't got a handy tree.)
Lots of room
To play
1 Pick up the tree trunk and cradle one end in your hands.
2 Throw the caber as far as you can.
3 The caber must hit the ground with the end you are not holding and tilt forward.

41

To cheat

If you aren't strong enough to pick up a caber then you could try tossing the pencil. Real weeds can try tossing the matchstick.

Games you wouldn't want to play

The Scots in the Middle Ages could play a little bit rough. Do *not* try these games on your school playing fields...

Hunt the human

This sport was popular with the Earl of Buchan (1381–1424).

To play

Set fire to Rothiemurchus Forest. The fire will drive out any deer, wolves, wild boar and outlaws that live in the forest.
Have well–armed hunters waiting outside the forest.
Kill everything that flees from the fire.
Eat the deer and boar. Leave the dead outlaws for the wolves to eat.

Gory gladiators

Gladiator contests were popular in Roman times – men fighting to the death to entertain the crowds. But the idea didn't quite disappear when the Romans left. A thousand years later, at the end of the 1300s, two Scottish clans decided to have a gladiator contest to settle an argument. The Chattans and the Cummings were the rivals.

King Robert III (1337–1406) and a huge crowd gathered on the North Inch of Perth to watch two teams of 30 butcher each other.

The rules were agreed before they started:

~Rules~

- 30 men on each team
- Each man armed with a sword, a dagger, an axe, a crossbow with three bolts and a round leather shield
- No armour to be worn, only a short kilt
- No one retires and no one is taken prisoner
- The team that is exterminated to the last man is the loser

Trumpets blew and the contest began. Bagpipes played and spectators roared louder than at a Celtic-Rangers football match. The sport went on for a long time while the king and his subjects cheered for their favourites. The Chattans won with 11 of their 30 men still alive at the end. Some books say only *one* Chattan was killed. Of course 19 dead Chattans were on the winning side but did not join in the celebrations.

One of the Cummings clan escaped with his life by swimming across the River Tay.

The king paid over £14 for this entertainment. That works out at about 35p a corpse.

Did you know...?

The Romans never conquered Scotland but they captured some very nice Caledonian bears. These were sent back to entertain people in the Circus at Rome. But it wasn't the big top type of circus with clowns. It was the Roman Circus where men and animals fought to the death to entertain the bloodthirsty crowds.

Battling bravehearts – The Middle Ages

Battling bravehearts timeline

1070 Vicious King Malcolm III meets Saxon Princess Margaret when a storm drives their ships into Wearmouth in Durham. She changes the Scottish church from loosely Christian to strict Roman Catholic.

1071 William the Conqueror invades and makes Malcolm and Scotland his subjects. This doesn't stop Malcolm raiding England when he feels like it.

1173 King William, the Lion of Scotland, is caught by English knights when he gets lost in a fog near Alnwick. He has to promise to obey the English king.

1286 Alexander III falls off a cliff and dies. Then the infant queen Margaret dies and 13 people claim the Scottish throne. One of them is Edward I of England. And he has an army to back him up. Edward becomes known as 'the hammer of the Scots'. Big man, big trouble.

1297 William Wallace leads a rebellion to throw the English out of Scotland. He loses and is executed in 1305.

1306 Robert the Bruce takes over the fight against the English. He

wins a lot of battles, especially…

1314 The Battle of Bannockburn. Edward II of England is smashed.

1320 Declaration of Arbroath by earls and barons says, 'It is freedom alone that we fight for.' They also warn Robert the Bruce they'll throw him out if he ever accepts English rule. Tough talk.

1328 Edward III of England agrees to let Scotland be free of English rule. Robert the Bruce rules, OK?

1329 *Not* OK. Robert dies and five-year-old David II takes over for 42 years – when he's not fleeing to France (1333–1341) or defeated and imprisoned by the English (1346–1357). The Plague arrives to cheer everyone up.

1371 Robert II takes the Scottish crown. He is the first of the famous Stuart kings. A writer says, 'There were horrible destructions, burnings and slaughters throughout the kingdom.' Nothing unusual, then.

1406 James I is captured by the English and held prisoner for 17 years.

1411 One of Scotland's bloodiest battles is fought at Harlaw. But it's Highland Scots attacking Lowland Scots. The Lowlanders win.

1437 King James I is murdered. James is not a lucky name for Scottish kings, but they don't learn.

1457 James II passes a law banning *futeball* in Scotland.

1460 James II tries to play *futeball* with a cannonball at the siege of Roxburgh – and loses.

1483 James III likes commoners around him. Lords hang his favourites over a bridge.

1488 James III accused of liking Englishmen now. This time it is James who gets the chop at Battle of Sauchieburn.

1496 Cruel new law *forces* sons of wealthy Scots to go to school!

Hammer Ed

The trouble with the Scottish wars in the Middle Ages was that they weren't played by the usual rules.

Scotland was left with a choice of 13 possible kings in 1286 when Alexander III died. The Scots made the mistake of asking King Edward I of England to judge who should get the crown. Edward chose John Balliol, an English baron, for the Scottish throne. Surprise, surprise!

Then, after four years, Balliol got a bit big for his boots and refused to do what Edward told him. So Edward marched up to Scotland with an army to show Balliol who was boss.

Edward became known as 'the hammer of the Scots' for his actions. Big Ed started with the Border town of Berwick. Forget the rules. He...

- burned the town
- killed the men, the women and the children
- ordered that the bodies should be left in the streets so the stench would remind the Scots of his power.

When Ed caught up with John Balliol in church he snatched the crown off the Scottish king's head and threw it to the soldiers to play with. Ed announced that he would take the throne of Scotland for himself.

The Scottish chiefs, bishops and lords were all ordered to go to smelly Berwick to sign a document and say they agreed. The document was known as 'The Ragman's Roll' – a 'ragman', like a miserable Scottish lord of the time, being a beggar.

Scotland was at an all time low. And then, along came William Wallace to lead them against Ed's evil English.

The Flying Scotsperson

11 September 1297   **5 Groats**

WALLACE WALLOPS ENGLISH
BROKEN BRIDGE NOBBLES KNIGHTS

William Wallace scored a shock victory over the arrogant English knights. The English crossed the little wooden bridge to where the Scots waited on the slopes of Abbey Craig. But there was no way back when the bridge collapsed. That was the sign for the gallant Scottish spear-men to rush down the hill and strike the mighty knights from their saddles. Scottish spears and Scottish hearts overcame the power of the English swords and battle-axes.

Wallace has been named 'Guardian of Scotland'. If Edward has any sense he'll stay out of our glorious country for good.

Of course it was too good to last. Within a year Edward I led an army personally to sort out the rebellious Scots. William Wallace told his men, 'I have led you into the ring, now see if you can dance.' But the only dance they were going to do was the dance of death. Wallace's army was shattered and he fled.

Wallace was betrayed and executed in 1304, but Edward died in 1307 and Wallace's friend, Robert the Bruce, had the chance to battle against the English.

The Bannock Bugle - late knight extra

Price: 2 groats   Date: 24 June 1314

ROBERT ROUTS RAIDERS
BRUCE BATTERS BOHUN

It was the match of the century at Bannockburn today when 7,000 Scots faced a mighty English army of over 20,000 – and won a famous victory. King Robert set the tone with a smashing success in single combat. As he rode at the head of his troops the big-headed English knight, de Bohun, charged him with his lance. The crafty king ducked and as the knight rode past, Robert split the English skull with his axe. 'That was my best axe and I snapped the handle!' Rob roared. That was all the encouragement our brave lads needed to savage the southerners.

Every Scot on the battlefield was a hero today. The English chargers died on the pikes of the Scottish foot-soldiers. A witness says that 'blood lay in pools on the ground'. Victory was Scotland's when English Edward II turned and ran away and his cowardly crew ran after him. They left a fortune in loot for the super Scottish slayers.

Luckless leaders

Life was miserable for Scottish monarchs. When they weren't killing somebody with cruelty they were being killed. It makes you wonder why anyone would *want* to be a Scottish king or queen!

Here are a few of the horrible highlights (or should that be lousy low-lights?).

Name: William Wallace

Life: 1270–1305

William Wallace was a war leader and 'Guardian of the throne' though he was never a crowned king. But his horrible story is important enough to put alongside the monarchs'.

Claim to fame:

- When Edward I of England tried to crush Scotland it was Wallace who led the rebellion against him. He defeated the English at Stirling Bridge.
- Wallace never had the support of all the great Scottish lords because he was not from a great family himself. In fact some of those lords wanted peace with England.
- Wallace lost the Battle of Falkirk, fled to France and gave up his post as Guardian. The Scottish lords made peace with England and Wallace returned from France to find he had few friends. Today he is remembered as one of Scotland's greatest heroes.

Cruel king: There was an English story that said Wallace defeated Hugh Cressingham in the Battle of Stirling Bridge. The Scots leader stripped the skin off Cressingham and made it into a belt for his sword. Other bits of skin were turned into girths for the Scottish horses or sent around Scotland to boast of the victory.

Of course the skinning of Cressingham could just be an English horror story. But it is true that the English Sheriff of Clydesdale torched Wallace's house and Wallace's revenge was to murder him. (See what happens when you play with fire?)

Funny fact: The story of Wallace's fighting life and dreadful death was made into a popular film in 1996. The film, *Braveheart*, made Scottish history popular around the world. But the film was made by Americans, William Wallace was played by an Australian and it was filmed largely in Ireland.

G'DAY YOU BLOKES! LET'S GO WALLOP SOME POMMIES! WHADYA RECKON?

Fantastic fact: Wallace was safe in his stronghold and the English were unable to reach him. They built a huge bonfire in sight of Wallace's fortress and brought out the wife of a Scottish lord. They threatened to throw her onto the fire. Wallace called them cowards and charged out from the safety of his castle to rescue her.

Foul fact: Wallace was betrayed. A Scots traitor called Monteith told him the Scottish authorities wanted him to promise peace. The giant Wallace allowed himself to be bound and handed over. The Scottish authorities handed him straight over to the avenging English king, Edward I.

Edward gave Wallace a sort of trial and sentenced him to die horribly. He was strapped to a gate, naked and head down, and pulled by a horse for two miles to the gallows. Even though his head was dragged over the ground he was still conscious when he was hanged by the neck. Before he was strangled he was cut down and his belly cut open. His bowels were ripped out and burned, then his heart was torn out. The arms and legs were cut off his body and sent to decorate castles in England and Scotland as a warning to rebels. His head was hung from the tower of London Bridge.

Name: Robert Bruce (or Robert the Bruce)

Life: 1274–1329

Claim to fame:

- Robert the Bruce took over as rebel leader when William Wallace died and he had himself crowned king.
- His greatest stroke of luck was that Edward I died soon after Robert came to the throne. He was left to face the feeble Edward II.
- The Scottish king defeated the English king at the Battle of Bannockburn in 1314 and won the right of Scotland to be free of English rule.

Cruel king: Robert the Bruce had a great rival for the Scottish throne, John Comyn of Badenoch. They made a deal – Bruce would have the crown but Comyn could have the lands. Seemed fair enough. But Comyn went running to Edward and said, 'Bruce is claiming to be king of Scotland.' Edward was furious and vowed revenge.

Bruce was annoyed that Comyn had split on him. So, he agreed to meet Comyn at the church of Grey Friars in Dumfries to make peace. Unfortunately Comyn laughed at Bruce's complaints. Bad-tempered Bruce stuck his dagger in Comyn and that stopped him from laughing.

Bloodstained Bruce rushed from the church. 'I'm afraid I've stabbed Comyn!'

His friend, Kirkpatrick, said, 'Don't be afraid – I'll go and make sure.' Kirkpatrick went and finished off the dying man.[1]

Bruce got himself crowned very quickly before news reached the Pope of his murdering a man in a church. (He knew the Pope would ban him from religious services like being crowned in a church.)

Funny fact: Robert wanted to be crowned properly, by the highest lord in the land. But the highest lord, the Earl of MacDuff, was just a child. The next best thing was the Earl's sister, the Countess of Buchan. She happened to be a cousin of the man Bruce had murdered and she didn't turn up for the ceremony. He had himself crowned anyway.

1. The motto of the Kirkpatrick family is still, 'I make sure.'

But then the Countess of Buchan turned up a day late (perhaps she'd missed her bus). He decided to be crowned by her after all and went through the coronation again. Robert is the only person to have been crowned king of Scotland *twice*!

And the poor Countess was later taken prisoner by the furious King of England. For helping crown Robert she was hung in an open cage over the walls of Berwick Castle for five years. She survived.

Fantastic fact: Robert was hunted by the English as well as by the powerful friends and family of murdered Comyn. He spent years battling to win his kingdom. There is the famous story about how Bruce spent one night, cold and tired, hiding in a cave in the Galloway Hills. He was ready to give up.

Then, by the light of his fire, he saw a spider swinging backwards and forwards from the ceiling, trying to reach the wall. It failed time and time again. At last it succeeded. 'If a spider can try and try again, then so can I!' Bruce cried. He carried on and was greeted by the news that Edward I, 'the hammer of the Scots', had died. (Do *not* try and copy the spider yourself. Swinging from the ceiling can damage the light fittings.)

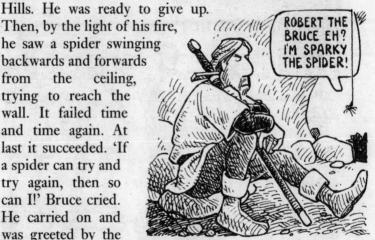

Foul fact: Many people believe that Robert the Bruce died of leprosy, but his friends visited him right up till his death on 7 June 1329. Would *they* have risked catching leprosy? Or did he die of some other disease?

Robert had one great ambition, to fight in the Holy Land

in a crusade against the Muslims. When he knew he was going to die he ordered that his heart should be removed from his corpse and be sent on a crusade. Sir James Douglas took the heart in a silver box, but his army was massacred before it reached the Holy Land and Robert never got his dying wish.

His body was buried in Dunfermline Abbey but it was lost 200 years later when Protestants wrecked the Abbey. In 1818 Robert the Bruce's skeleton was found – with his chest bone sawn through where the heart was taken out – and given a second burial. His heart, on the other hand, was buried 50 miles away in Melrose. In 1996 it was dug up, but not unwrapped from its lead casing – that would have been a heartless thing to do!

Names: James I, II, III, IV and V

Claims to fame:
- James was not a lucky name for Scottish kings and most died strange, violent, or tragic deaths.
- The last four all became king when they were children – which meant violence in Scotland as grown-ups fought to control them (and their fortune).
- James I was a prisoner in England for 17 years after being captured by English pirates. He returned to

Scotland in 1424 and began to sort out the squabbling barons.

Cruel kings: while James I had been a prisoner in England, he reckoned the Scottish lords hadn't done enough to set him free. When he returned he had them executed. His cruellest act was to give his son the unlucky name – James!

James II was six years old when he came to the throne and quickly learned to be ruthless – he witnessed a murder when he was nine years old in 1440. Twelve years later he was having dinner at Stirling with the Earl of Douglas. Suddenly James II drew his knife and stabbed his guest. The Earl wasn't dead – at least not until the servants finished him off for their king. They beat his brains out with a pole-axe.[1] Then he went and named his son James.

James III had an enemy, the Earl of Mar. James had him arrested. Next thing, Mar bled to death. No one quite knows how but he didn't cut his finger opening a can. James is suspected of having something to do with it.

James IV was at the head of the army that defeated and killed his own father. He was sorry about this, in fact he was so upset that he punished himself by wearing a heavy chain round his waist for the rest of his life. As he grew

1. Parliament said Douglas was to blame for his own death, not the King. They said, if Douglas had done what the King wanted then James wouldn't have had to kill him. Hmmm!

older, and fatter, new links had to be added to the chain.

James V became king at the age of one. He controlled the wild Highlanders by taking many of their chiefs prisoner. He said, 'I have a list of 300 nobles that I can hang whenever I wish.' He was not a popular man – well, not with the 300 nobles on his list.

Funny facts: James III was unusual because he surrounded himself with commoners for friends. The Scottish nobles were jealous and took their revenge. They captured the King's favourite, a stonemason called Cochrane, and threw him over a bridge with a rope round his neck as the young King was forced to watch. The nobles then kept James III as their prisoner. He was released by his brother and said, 'Thanks, brother!' by trying to poison him! (The brother died soon after when a splintered lance killed him as he was watching a joust between two knights.)

James IV was a great one for investigating things. He agreed to meet an Italian priest who claimed he had wings that would fly him all the way to France. The priest jumped off the roof of Stirling Castle ... and flew all the way down to the castle dung heap. (He blamed the chicken feathers in the wings: 'Chickens are attracted to dung heaps.') James helped to patch up the priest's broken leg and made him an abbot. James IV also fancied himself as a doctor and liked to practise on his citizens. The king paid one man 14 shillings (70p) to let him take all his teeth out.

There are stories (not proved) that James V liked to wander through Scotland disguised as a beggar. That way he could find out what they were saying about him. It is possible that he really went around looking for young ladies to chat up because he was a terrible flirt.

Fantastic fact: James IV had a ghostly warning that he would die if he invaded England. He went to the chapel in his palace at Linlithgow that summer, and was surrounded by all his lords. As he prayed, the church door opened. A strange figure stood in the doorway: a man in a blue gown

with hair down to his shoulders and a high, bald forehead. He was a ghastly, pale man of about 50 years and he carried a pike-staff in his hand. He stepped forward and said, 'Sir, I am sent to warn you not to go where you plan. If you do then you will not do well and the people with you will suffer!' Then the figure vanished. Sir David Lindsay and Sir John Inglis, who were standing by the King reached forward to grab the man and question him. But even

though he was standing between them they could not lay a hand on him before he vanished. Some people have said this was a trick that Queen Margaret arranged to stop her husband from invading England. But, if it was, no one can say how it was arranged. What's more, it failed. James vowed to go on ... and he died in the battle.

Foul facts: James I was the first Scottish king to be murdered since the Dark Ages. Eight assassins arrived at the monastery where James was staying. His own cousins unlocked the doors to them – you can't trust anyone. James heard the murderers coming and used a poker to raise a floorboard and slip down into the sewers. In order to help him, his wife and her maidservants tried to bar the door. They were injured as the eight men burst in. Sadly King James was just too fat to squeeze through the sewers. He was dragged out and hacked to death.

James II died just as messily. He was killed in 1460 when he was having a siege at Roxburgh Castle. He ordered the firing of his cannon to welcome his wife to the siege. One cannon exploded and blew him up. He had a red birthmark on his face that gave him the nickname 'fiery face'. But not so fiery as it was after the cannon blast, of course. He'd have been pleased to know that his forces captured the castle!

James III found himself in a battle against his nobles, the English ... and his own son! He fell off his horse as he escaped and was carried to a mill to rest. James III asked the miller to fetch a priest to pray for him. The priest asked a passing group of knights to help. One said he would see to the King. In fact the 'priest' was Lord Gray, James's enemy, who drew a dagger and stabbed the King to death.

James IV invaded England. Most of the English army was in France so he thought it would be easy. He had a huge force of around 60,000 men. It's said that the day before the battle he went off flirting with English Lady Heron and she persuaded him to take off his lucky chain. Without it his army were massacred – 10,000 died – and he was cut to pieces on the battlefield.

James V had a very powerful Border lord called Johnnie Armstrong. Johnnie ruled his land like a king and other lords were jealous of his power. They persuaded James V to get rid of Johnnie Armstrong, but he did it in a very cowardly way. If he'd marched in with an army then Johnnie would have fought back with his own army. So James tricked Johnnie. He invited him to come hunting with just three dozen Armstrong men. The King turned up with a small army and hanged the lot of them. Years later he hadn't the courage to lead his army against a full English force. He sent a leaderless army to fight and they were defeated. James, aged just 30, gave up on life, lay down on his bed and simply died. His throne passed to his daughter, Mary Queen of Scots, who was just six days old at the time.

Wild women and crazy cures

The men of Scotland are supposed to be full of fighting spirit. The warrior women had to be just as tough. Here are a few of the thousands who deserve to be remembered...

Fighting females

Black Agnes

The Countess of Dunbar held Dunbar Castle against the English attackers for 19 weeks in 1338. The English smashed her walls with huge catapults. Agnes walked along the top of the castle wall and looked at the scarred walls. Just to annoy the English she dusted the scars with a white handkerchief!

Then the English attacked with battering rams – Agnes ordered that the broken walls should be thrown down on top of the batterers. The English gave up and went home.

Kate Douglas

When assassins came to murder James I, his door should have been barred with a beam of wood held in two sockets. Then the only way to break in would have been to charge till they shattered the beam. But the beam had been stolen by plotters inside the house. To give James a chance to escape, the Queen's waiting-woman, Kate Douglas, jammed her arm in the sockets. Now the only way for the attackers to get in the room was to charge till they shattered her arm ... which they did. She got the nickname

Kate Bar-lass after that. There are still people in Scotland named Barlas after her – but don't ask them if it's because their granny worked in a bar![1]

Queen Joan

James I's wife, Joan, had the pleasure of capturing his killers and their leader, Walter, Earl of Atholl. She could have had him hanged, drawn and quartered, but she wanted a more savage revenge than that. She made his execution last three days. On the first day he had a rope tied round his feet and was hoisted into the air on a crane. The rope was allowed to drop towards the ground then stopped suddenly so his legs were pulled out of their sockets. He was then led off to a pillory and crowned with a red-hot iron crown that was stamped 'king of traitors'. On the second day he was dragged through the streets of Edinburgh, strapped to a stretcher that was tied to the tail of a horse. James I's loyal subjects could jeer and throw things at him. Only on the third day was he finally hanged, drawn and quartered. The message was, 'Don't mess with Joan!'

I NEVER THOUGHT I'D BE SO GLAD TO SEE *YOU*

1. Some boring people say Kate Bar-lass wasn't even in the room at the time she was supposed to have struggled to save the King. Pity, because it's a good story!

Mary of Gueldres

 James II's wife was a tough woman who went to war with him. When he was blown up by a cannon she could have given up and gone home. Instead she carried on with the battle to take Roxburgh Castle and won it for her son, James III. She then led a force to capture other English castles at Wark and Norham. She went back home and built Ravenscraig Castle, the first Scottish castle to be built with extra strength roofing to take cannon. After a series of boyfriends she fancied being a queen again so she proposed to Edward IV of England shortly before she died!

The lady of Skibo Castle

 In the 1650s the Earl of Montrose fought to keep Scotland for Charles II. After some great successes Montrose was at last captured. His enemies treated him dreadfully. The Earl was dressed in peasant rags, tied to an old horse and led south. When his captors reached Skibo Castle the lady of the house expected the Earl to have the seat of honour at her table. Instead General Holbourn, the commander of the guards, took the seat. The lady told the general to move. He refused, so she picked up a steaming leg of roast lamb and smashed it over the general's head. (Sadly, the Earl was executed, and leg of Montrose ended up hanging from castles in Scotland. When Charles returned 11 years later, Montrose's enemy was executed at the same spot.)

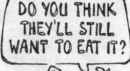 DO YOU THINK THEY'LL STILL WANT TO EAT IT?

Lady Seaforth

 In 1578 Lord Seaforth went to France. A fortune-teller, Sallow Kenneth, went to Lady Seaforth and told her that her husband was flirting with other women in France. Did she punish Lord Seaforth? No. She punished fortune-teller Kenneth instead. She had him popped into a tar barrel lined with spikes. It was set on fire and rolled down a hill. He was a bit upset, to say the least. As he died, he cursed the family and told them they would die horribly. And they did – but not as horribly as Kenneth, you can be sure.

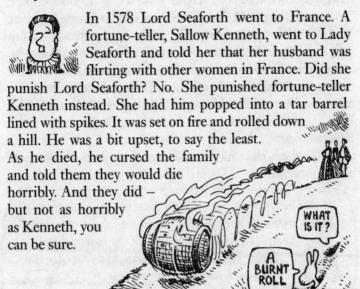

WHAT IS IT?

A BURNT ROLL

Flattened females

Of course women were often the victims of violence too...

Katherine Mortimer

 In 1357 King David II owed Edward of England £100,000 and took the money from his lords. Instead of giving the money to Edward he spent it on his girlfriends. The most expensive girlfriend was Katherine Mortimer. One of David's lords was furious at the way she spent the money. He attacked her on the road at Soutra Hill and stabbed her to death.

Lady Margaret Drummond

King James IV fell in love with Margaret Drummond and wanted to marry her. There had been two queens in the Drummond

63

family before and she would have been a good choice. Someone disagreed. Margaret died suddenly one morning in 1502. Since her sister died at the same time it's a fair bet they were the victims of a poisoner ... which is a bit rough on Margaret's sister who just happened to be in the wrong place at the wrong time. (When James was 28 he married 13-year-old Margaret, the sister of Henry VIII.)

Did you know...?
In 1703 the writer Martin Martin described a custom in the Western Isles...

> *It was an ancient custom for a man to take a woman to be his wife and keep her for a year without marrying her. If she pleased him all the while, he married her at the end of the year. But, if he did not love her, he returned her to her parents.*

You'll notice the poor woman had no say in the matter!

Margaret MacLeod was sent back to her family this way in 1600. During her year with Donald Gorm she damaged her eye and he wanted a refund – as you would if your new car had a damaged headlight! Gorm packed her off on a one-eyed horse led by a one-eyed groom and a one-eyed dog. Margaret's family were furious and a two-year war broke out. It was known as the War of the One-eyed Woman.

Crazy cures

If you cured sickness then there was a chance that you'd be accused of witchcraft. How could the people of old Scotland tell? The cures they tried were so weird they may as well have waved a magic wand.

Many villages had a 'wise woman' who would know these old cures and only pass them on when she was dying.

If a wise woman had been kind enough to write it down then her remedy book may have looked something like this...

Dear Villagers
   I, Mad Meg, being of sound mind, leave these clever cures for you good people to practise.
   ..~~..
• Does your husband suffer from baldness? Then burn pigeon droppings and rub the ashes into the scalp to cure it.

• Gout can be very painful, I know. But in the 1600s they said that to cure gout you should take the skin from the feet of a large vulture and wrap it round the heel. There's not a lot of vultures round these parts so I prefer their other cure. They say you can boil a frog in olive oil and rub the liquid on a gouty foot.

• Do you suffer from pain? One day someone will invent aspirin. Meanwhile, to take away pain, shoot an arrow from east to west. As the arrow disappears, so will the pain. (Unless you hit someone, of course.)

• I'll never forget this story my granny told me. She said that the Bishop of St Andrews in the 1500s was seriously ill. He was hung upside down for a week and fed the flesh of puppy dogs. He recovered. Of course, the puppies didn't. I'm not in favour of cruelty to animals, but I do know that in the 1600s the wise women of Scotland believed that the best way to cure a raging fever was to throw a cat over the sick person.

• Herbs and plants are much kinder.
You just have to remember, treat like
with like. Trouble with the blood?
Blood is red, so drink beetroot juice.
And rhubarb is wonderful (never mind
the custard)

• Now, I know some of you have trouble
sleeping. When that happens to me I try
eating nettles mixed with the white of an
egg. (My dad always said, 'Sleep on the
edge of the bed and you'll soon drop off,'
but he was a bit soft in the head.)

• There are people who have fits, but I have
a certain cure. Mark the spot where the
first fit happened and bury a black
cockerel there – alive. Of course it'll soon
be dead. Some of you might like to dig it
up and use the skull as a drinking cup.
This cures all sorts of illnesses.

• Young girls who want to make
themselves beautiful should wash their
face in goat's milk. Drinking it also cures a

hangover if you've had too much wine —
but fathers beware — don't drink the
stuff your ugly daughter's just washed
her face in!

• Then there's toothache. Just take an
iron nail and drill it into the gum where
it hurts till there's blood on the end.
Drive the nail into an oak tree and the
toothache will be cured.

• And finally a warning. Everyone knows
that a brew made from foxgloves can
cure heart disease. I want to tell you that
I tried it. It worked. So I took some
more. But too much will pois-

These old country cures sound silly. But even respectable
doctors had strange ideas. In 1796, the poet Robbie Burns
was ill with rheumatic fever and his doctor told him that
sea-bathing, in the chilly Solway Firth, would cure him.
It actually helped to kill him.

Tudor terrors – the 1500s

While the Tudors were hacking heads in England, the Scots were doing pretty bloody things too. Any excuse to splash a bit of gore. Excuses like...

- The Border region between the two countries was a lawless battle zone ruled by thieves – rival gangs fought law officers and each other.
- Henry VIII seemed to hate the Scots because he enjoyed having people to hate, and they were his neighbours. He sent armies to batter the Scots.
- Scots began cruel killings as the new Protestant religion began pushing the old Catholic religion out. Catholics and Protestants burned, chopped and hanged one another.
- Children inherited the Scottish throne and lords butchered rivals to control them.

All in all a horrible historical time to live in Scotland.

Tudor timeline

1503 James IV of Scotland marries fat Henry VIII's sister from England, Margaret. This should unite the nations. Fat chance.

1513 The Battle of Flodden. Henry VIII sends an army to defeat the Scots. James IV dies in the battle.

1542 James V's troops lose to the English at Solway Moss and he dies of a broken heart. His six-day-old daughter, Mary Queen of Scots, takes the crown (even though it's too big for her).

1544 Henry VIII of England sends troops to batter the Borderers, which becomes known as the 'rough

wooing'. Scots unite against England.

1559 John Knox leads Scottish 'reformation', bringing in the Protestant religion and wrecking Catholic churches and monasteries.

1561 Mary Queen of Scots returns to Scotland where her mother has been ruling till young Mary grew up. Now is the time of plotting and murder, rebellion and civil war.

1567 Mary Queen of Scots is thrown off the throne and flees to England. She asks cousin Queen Elizabeth I of England to protect her. Liz 'protects' Mary for 19 years in prison! In Scotland her 13-month-old son, James VI, becomes king.

1587 Elizabeth I finally decides to execute Mary Queen of Scots. Liz says sorry to James, so that's all right.

1590 Start of the North Berwick witch trials; torture and terror for many innocent people in Scotland.

1603 James VI of Scotland takes the throne of England too when Elizabeth dies and becomes James I of England. Finally, one king for both countries. Peace at last? No chance.

The Hornshole horror

James IV was defeated at the Battle of Flodden in 1513 and Scotland was wide open to an invasion. The Highlanders were safe enough back in the mountains and the Lowlanders could retreat to their castles. It was the people in the Border towns who faced the greatest danger of attack.

Many of the Border men had died at Flodden and an English army was on its way. The town of Selkirk sent hundreds of men to Flodden – only the town clerk returned alive.

Who was left to defend the nearby town of Hawick when the English marched towards them? Just the ones who were too young to fight at Flodden.

If one of the boys of Hawick had kept a diary in 1514 it may have looked something like this...

– Dear diary –

My name is Tam Stirk. This is the first day of my diary and I'm afraid it could well be my last. The English are coming from Hexham, burning every house and murdering every person in their way. My mam says she won't let them hurt her wee Tam. I'm not sure how she's going to stop them

– Day 2 –

They're in Teviotdale now. I thought I'd be dead, but the English are slow because they're stopping to eat and drink everything they lay their hands on. My mam says they won't get their hands on her porridge.

(Actually, a dose of mam's porridge would probably kill them. It's horrible, but I daren't tell her.) Iain Nixon says there's a meeting of all the lads of Hawick at the Market Cross at noon today. I may as well go along.

— Later in Day 2 —

That was great! Young Iain stood at the foot of the cross and said, 'Are we going to sit here and let the English murder us in our beds?' 'No!' we all cried. (It was dead exciting.) 'Are we going to run away and let them burn our homes?' 'Yes!' I cried. Then I noticed everybody else was shouting 'No!' 'So what are we going to do?' he cried. 'I don't know!' I shouted back. But the others were shouting, 'Attack them!' It seems the drunken English are camped at Hornshole. When it gets dark, the lads are going to jump on them and chop them up! I'll go along but, knowing my luck. I'll be the one that gets chopped. Goodbye, diary.

— Day 3 —

Would you believe it? I'm alive. Covered in blood, but alive because it's English blood. The boys collected every weapon they could find – knives and hay-forks, corn flails and axes or big lumps of wood. The English didn't even have guards when we got to their camp. We just marched in. The lads stabbed the ones on the ground asleep and the ones that were awake were too drunk to fight. I hit one with my mam's porridge pan but I think he was already dead.

When we left we took the blue and gold Hexham flag and there wasn't a single Englishman left alive. I told

> my mam that I'm a hero. She says, 'I'm proud of you, son ... but I'll never get that English blood out of your best shirt!'

The victory of the Hawick boys is still celebrated every year, when the flag is paraded round the town. The people of Hawick are so proud of their history they have a famous saying…

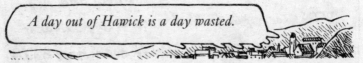

A day out of Hawick is a day wasted.

Rotten religions

Religion has been an important part of Scotland's history since the prehistoric Picts. When the Protestant ideas arrived in the early 1500s it was the start of a long and bloody battle that is still going on in some parts of Scotland today…

Battering Beaton

David Beaton (1494–1546) was a Catholic bishop at a time when the Protestants were making a nuisance of themselves. He burned 11 of them – meanwhile, over the border in England, Henry VIII was burning almost 11,000 people for religious crimes, so Beaton wasn't such a Tudor terror.

Still, he had his enemies. And they got him in the end. His murder in 1546 is one of the most dramatic in Scotland's long list of murders…

THEY FINISHED STABBING HIM AND HUNG HIM OUT OF THE WINDOW BY ONE ANKLE, STILL NAKED

HE HAS A GOOD VIEW OF THE SPOT WHERE HE BURNED OUR FRIEND GEORGE WISHART

Poaching Patrick

When Patrick Hamilton was executed in 1528 for being a Protestant, he wasn't the only person to be burned. One of the Catholic monks who went to jeer Hamilton had a small accident. If he'd written to his abbot then the letter may have looked like this...

Dear Abbot,

I am sending this written report on my visit to Edinburgh as I am too poorly to return to the monastery just now. I have been burned while watching the execution of Patrick Hamilton. I'm not as badly burned as Patrick Hamilton, of course (if you'll excuse my little joke!).

The man admitted that he'd been to Wittenberg and met the Protestant devil Martin Luther. Then he came back to Scotland and started preaching Luther's filth. The Catholic bishops tricked Hamilton into a meeting at St Andrews and put him on trial. He was guilty, of course, and sent to the stake.

The kind bishops gave him the chance to repent. He was brought to the stake outside the college of St Andrews. 'Throw a burning stick onto the wood pile. It's a sign that you are sorry and we can let you live.'

What did Hamilton say? He said, 'No!' The kind bishops just had to burn him, didn't they? I mean, he asked for it. Sadly he didn't ask to be burned quite as slowly as he was. The wood was damp, you see.

The kind bishops had placed gunpowder in the pile and that exploded. It only scorched Hamilton's left hand and face. He called out for more gunpowder, but they only had more damp wood. Of course, a group of monks were marching round the fire, chanting, as we do, 'Repent!'

What did he say? He said, 'You're a bit late with that advice. If I was going to repent I wouldn't be here.'

The cheek! Anyway a baker felt sorry for him smouldering away so he brought a bale of straw and threw it on the fire to make it blaze. A gust of wind caught it and I was in exactly the wrong place. The blast of flame hit me in the face, singed my cowl and left me with no eyebrows or beard. And my nose is badly scorched, too.

They tell me they could still hear Hamilton praying. Someone called for him to give a sign of his faith and he managed to raise three fingers – for God the father, God the son and God the Holy Ghost, of course. They were still raised when the flames finally killed him.

As I was led away to the infirmary I heard a gentleman speaking to the Bishop of St Andrews. He said, 'If we burn any more, my Lord, then let them be burned in cellars. The smoke of Patrick Hamilton has affected as many as it has blown upon.'

And it certainly seems the Catholics lost a lot of friends today.

I'll be back when my hair grows back. Being burned is a painful business.

Brother Francis

Many Scots were turning away from the Catholic Church anyway. The death of Patrick Hamilton in 1528 drove many more to become Protestants. Then the trouble really started.

The Catholics and the Protestants couldn't agree to live in peace. They just had to fight one another, didn't they?

Did you know...?
The rival religions took each other very seriously. In 1688 an Aberdeen Catholic insulted the local Protestants by naming his two dogs after Protestant heroes, Calvin and Luther. The poor dogs were arrested and hanged at the Market Cross! (If Ford Motor Company took over Britain would they hang every dog called Rover?)

Mad about Mary

Mary Queen of Scots returned to Scotland as queen when her mother died. But 19-year-old Mary was Catholic and Scotland had turned Protestant while she'd been away.

Her leading enemy was the Protestant leader, John Knox – a hard man who didn't think much of women and thought even less of Mary. Mary and Knox had a meeting and Knox, very kindly, said Mary could stay on the throne ... so long as she didn't try to turn Scotland back into a Catholic country. In spite of this bit of cheek, Knox was not executed.

(BUT ... don't worry, lots of other people died horribly during Mary's lifetime so there's lots of bloody history to hear about.)

Knox found it was possible to be Mary's enemy and live. A lot of men found it was possible to love Mary and *die…*

Mad about Mary – 1

Many Scottish lords became Protestant because it gave them a chance to grab more power. But the Earl of Huntly stayed loyal. 'I'll bring the Catholic Church back to three counties!' he boasted. Then he suggested that Mary might like to marry his son, John Gordon. Brilliant idea! Powerful Catholic lord for a father-in-law and a handsome Catholic husband.

What did Mary decide to do?

a) Make Huntly her chief minister and marry John Gordon.
b) Make Huntly her chief minister but not marry John Gordon.
c) Go to war with Huntly and execute John Gordon.

Answer: Obviously, c) is quite stupid, you'll agree. So, as you guessed, Mary did c). Her force met Huntly's at the Battle of Corrichie – Catholic Scot against Catholic Scot – John Knox and his Protestants must have loved that!

Old Huntly had a fit, fell out of the saddle and died on the spot. His son, Sir John, was captured and led away for execution. Mary decided to watch and Sir John was delighted. 'I am comforted by you being here, Queen Mary!' he cried. 'I am dying for love of you!'

That upset Mary a bit. But the botched-up butchery of the execution upset her more. She wept and had to be carried back to her room. (So did Sir John, of course, but he never recovered from the execution.)

Have you spotted what is missing from between the capture of Sir John to his execution? Yes, a trial! And that's the really, *really* horrible historical bit of the case.

He had to be tried so he could be found guilty and be sentenced to have his lands taken off him. So, he was put back together and his dead body was taken to court and tried.

Mary gave most of the Huntly lands to her stepbrother, who became the Earl of Moray. More about him later.

Mad about Mary – 2

Some people never learn. After executing Sir John she went south again and stopped at Burntisland Castle. A French poet called Chastelard was in love with Mary. He found the room she'd be sleeping in, crept inside and hid under her bed.

Then he was dragged

out and about to be stabbed by the guards. The Earl of Moray stopped them and insisted on giving Chastelard a trial – while he was still alive.

Of course he was sentenced to death and, of course, Mary watched the sport. And, of course, the poet cried, 'I am dying for love of you, my most beautiful and cruel queen in the world.' (This is getting to be a bit of a habit, you may notice.)

Being a poet he could have done better. Maybe…

ROSES ARE RED,
VIOLETS ARE BLUE;
I WISH I COULD
STICK MY HEAD ON WITH GLUE

Mad about Mary – 3

Everybody agreed that Queen Mary needed a husband. The trouble was she was bad at picking her feller. (She

should have stuck to picking her nose.) Her first husband had been the king of France. He didn't last long, but at least he died of natural causes. I suppose it's natural to die when your head's lopped off.

Next she fell for her handsome cousin, Henry Darnley, and married the young man. He was a spoilt brat. He didn't just want to be the Queen's husband. He wanted to be called 'king' and he turned very stroppy until Mary finally said 'Yes'. Still, she was getting fed up with Darnley and that meant murder.

Then Mary got herself a new boyfriend, James, the Earl of Bothwell. And someone plotted to blow up Darnley in his Edinburgh house. The plot did not go quite according to plan. Historians have many clues and have argued for centuries about what happened that night in Kirk o' Fields house.

If you were the famous Scottish detective, Sherlock McHolmes, would you be able to sort out how Darnley died? Here is the evidence...

Sherlock

The bodies of Darnley and his servant, William Taylor, were found dead in the garden of Darnley's house. The house had been badly damaged by an explosion, followed by a fire. The bodies showed no signs of being burned. They were both dressed in nightshirts with Darnley's velvet robe beside him. There were marks round their necks which suggested they had been strangled. A velvet chair was on the grass by the bodies. A rope of bedclothes was fastened to the chair. I questioned all witnesses and suspects.

Widow McCutcheon

I am a neighbour of Lord Darnley and the Queen. I watched her ride away earlier this evening with Lord Bothwell, then went to bed after supper. In the middle of the night I heard horsemen and they seemed to have Lord Darnley's house surrounded. Then I heard a scream. It was his voice and he cried, 'Oh, my brothers, have pity on me for the love of Jesus who had mercy on all the world!' Then he went horribly quiet. I heard men running, then horses galloping away. About a minute later there was a terrible explosion like the sound of 30 cannon going off at once. I hope no one was hurt!

Thomas Nelson

I am a servant to Darnley. My Lord Darnley has been very ill lately but, with Queen Mary's care, he had begun to get better. Yesterday evening the Queen went off to a wedding party and he was very upset. Especially when she said she wouldn't be back that night. Lord Bothwell rode off with her. My Lord Darnley went to his bedroom after supper – William Taylor slept on the floor next to him while I slept outside the door. I woke to hear my Lord Darnley and William Taylor shouting in the room; the door was locked so I couldn't get in. Then they went quiet. I ran downstairs to see what was happening. As I reached the door there was an

explosion that blew me across the stable yard, but I survived. I was knocked unconscious but woke to hear people say Darnley and Taylor had been blown into the garden and killed.

Mary Queen of Scots

I had no idea this was going to happen. I could have been in there and died with my husband, Darnley. I must say, as I mounted my horse to leave last night, I noticed a man called Nicholas Herbert coming from the cellars and he was covered in grime. I see now that it must have been gunpowder and he had been filling the cellar with the stuff. I hope you don't think I had anything to do with my dear husband's death! Oh, I should mention, that Nicholas Herbert man is one of Lord Bothwell's servants!

Lord Bothwell

I met my Queen last night to escort her to the wedding party. I was at the party all night and I have witnesses who saw me there. I know Henry Darnley was a murderer but who on earth would want to blow him up? Don't worry about the Queen – I'll take good care of her!

Whodunnit?

Have you worked it out? Here's what most people believe…

- Mary and Bothwell plotted to kill Darnley by blowing him up as he slept.
- Bothwell arranged to have the cellars of the house packed with gunpowder.

- Bothwell escorted Mary from the house and told her it would be best for her to stay away that night.
- In the early hours, a party of horsemen arrived to light the fuse. NOTE: This was a *big* mistake. One man could have done it silently.
- The horsemen woke Darnley and he ran to the window and saw them.
- The fuse was lit and began to burn.
- William Taylor made a rope of sheets and lowered Darnley to the ground then let himself down. (Darnley was too ill to climb down himself.)
- The assassins caught Darnley in the garden and smothered him with his own nightgown. He only had time to cry out, 'Oh, my brothers, have pity on me for the love of Jesus who had mercy on all the world!'
- They killed the witness, William Taylor. They should have dragged the bodies back into the house to be destroyed. But the fuse was already burning.
- They left the bodies in the garden and fled just before the gunpowder exploded.

Bothwell was accused and summoned to a trial…

Not only did Bothwell get away with it … he also got to marry the Queen!

Mad about Mary – 4

One of Darnley's acts that upset Mary was that he was mixed up in the murder of her favourite secretary, a young Italian called David Riccio. This is one murder that *did* go to plan.

Mary was at dinner in her room with David Riccio and some friends for company. The door to her bedroom opened and Darnley stepped through. He'd come up the back stairway from his own room. Mary and Darnley had not been getting along too well lately, but now he put an arm around her. It seemed a friendly thing to do … but it was all part of the plot.

They heard the tramp of steel boots in the corridor outside. Then the main door to the room was flung open and Lord Ruthven stood there. He was a strange sight, for he was dressed in armour but wore his nightgown over the top. He spoke to the Queen, 'Let it please your Majesty, that David Riccio come out of your room.'

'What has he done?' Mary cried.

'He's offended your honour, stood in the way of Lord Darnley taking the crown, and many other things,' Ruthven replied.

Suddenly there was chaos in the room. A group of armed killers clattered into the room. Riccio rushed from his seat and clung to the Queen's skirts. She couldn't move to help because her husband, Darnley, tightened his grip on her shoulders. Riccio screamed, 'Save my life, my Lady, save my life!' His fingers were bent back and forced off Mary's skirts. He was dragged away from her.

Two men forced pistols against the Queen's side and warned her to stay still. Knives flashed in the firelight and struck at the screaming servant. One murderer snatched Darnley's own knife from its sheath and lunged at the Italian secretary. Mary felt the cold draught as the steel brushed past her face.

The victim was dragged from the room and the screaming soon stopped. He lay dead with 56 stab wounds on his body. One dagger was left in the corpse to show who was responsible. It was Darnley's dagger.

Darnley was clearly to blame for Riccio's murder – no doubt about that. But there is a mystery about this attack. Mary swore later that one of the men holding a gun to her side had pulled the trigger! The gun misfired and she was unhurt. Was the Queen of Scots meant to die in this incident? Or why would she lie?

Was Darnley brought to trial? Of course not. But Mary waited and plotted her own type of justice for her murdering husband. Scottish law couldn't touch him – Mary's revenge could.

Mad about Mary – 5

Mary and Bothwell were not a popular pair. Mary's stepbrother, Moray, returned to Scotland and defeated the killing couple in battle. Bothwell ran away (and didn't stop running till he got to Denmark!). Mary was captured and Moray said her son, James VI, would

now be king – Moray himself would be regent.

Mary was a problem, of course. What could Moray do with her? Mary solved his problem by escaping to England and asking Queen Elizabeth I for protection. Elizabeth had no children. If she died then cousin Mary would become Queen of England. (She'd already been Queen of France and Queen of Scotland so that would be quite a hat trick!)

People around Mary popped off like lemmings off a cliff. Elizabeth did what any sensible cousin would do. She locked her up – for 18 years!

Still men were going mad for Mary. A young page boy called Anthony Babington was mad for Mary when she was a prisoner. He grew up with a dream of setting her free and putting her on Elizabeth's throne. He never met her again, but she was the death of him, like all the others.

The trouble was that Elizabeth *wanted* someone to plot with Mary. She wanted an excuse to execute her problem cousin, Mary Queen of Scots. Elizabeth's spies heard about Anthony Babington's plot and helped him to write secret letters to Mary in her Chartley Castle prison. The spies were reading every letter and at last they got what they wanted. The letters went something like this…

6 July 1586

Your Gracious Majesty,
Since I know this letter will reach you safely I can reveal to you the details of my plot. It will be in four parts.
First, there will be an invasion of England by your Catholic allies from France and Spain.
Then, as they land, Catholic gentlemen of

England will take up arms to help the invaders.

Once we control the country you will be released from your prison.

Last, the Protestant queen on your throne will be despatched by a group of six of my most trusted friends.

We await your approval.

Your loyal servant,
Anthony Babington ...

The English spies read this but didn't arrest Babington yet. They sealed up the letter and passed it on to Mary. She replied...

17 July 1786

Sir Anthony

Thank you for your welcome letter. It raises my spirits and fills me with fear. If my rescue is delayed, and word reaches here of the plot, then my jailer will kill me. You must plan my rescue very carefully.

The invasion from Spain must also be timed very carefully and we need to be sure that the force is strong enough for victory. Let the great plot go ahead.

Mary, Queen of Scots

The letter showed she wanted to rebel against Elizabeth. It didn't say clearly that she wanted Elizabeth dead. So the spies added an extra paragraph to the letter before it was passed to Anthony Babington...

> P.S. I would like to know the names of the six gentlemen who would perform the deed. Tell me when the assassination will take place and how they will do it. M

Babington replied to the letter ... then he was arrested. When he was tortured in the Tower of London he admitted his part in the plot – wouldn't you? Like Mary's other young men he had a horrible historical end – hanged, drawn and quartered, just like William Wallace. But Babington was English, so it doesn't matter so much. As for Mary, it was the end. She was arrested, tried and found guilty. Her sentence was to be beheaded at Fotheringhay Castle in England.

Did you know...?
Catholic Mary's great Protestant enemy, John Knox, thought women were a bit wicked and wrote a document called, *The first blast of the trumpet against the monstrous regiment of women.* Most people think he was attacking Mary Queen of Scots in this. Actually it was aimed at Queen Mary I of England and French Mary of Guise. (Mary of Guise had had him arrested and made him serve 19 months as a galley slave.)

But, if Knox was such a woman-hater, how come he reached the age of 50 and married a 17-year-old girl?

Suffering school

The Scottish people are very proud of their education system. They are sure it is better than the one over the border in England. No one can agree on why this is…

BECAUSE SCOTTISH BAIRNS ARE BRAINIER!

BECAUSE SCOTTISH TEACHERS ARE BETTER

But teachers and pupils have to remember it hasn't always been cool at school for Scots.

As usual boys were the ones who got schools. Girls were mostly taught at home until the 1870s. But some of the schools were harsh places. Here are a few examples of the evils of education…

1546 George Wishart opposed the Catholic Church so Cardinal David Beaton had him burned at the stake. But that's all right. Wishart was only a school teacher so his pupils just had an extra day off school. Of course Beaton was murdered in revenge. Would anyone bother to avenge your teacher's death if they were burned at the stake?

1591 King James VI had terrible trouble with witches and uncovered a plot in North Berwick. When the witches were caught, the leading witch turned out to be a school master, John Fian. What's more, John Fian admitted it and was burned. (All right, so he was being tortured at the time. But this is no excuse for you to torture your teacher, even if you do suspect them of being a witch.)

1595 The pupils of Edinburgh High School were fed up because they had their holidays cut. They piled up stores of food in the school hall, gathered some weapons and barred the doors – they were having a 'lock in'. Now, your teachers would probably laugh and let you stay there. But the Edinburgh High staff called in the law officer, Bailie MacMorran. He sent men to batter down the doors. Pupil William Sinclair leaned out of the window, fired a pistol at the law men and killed Bailie MacMorran. Young Will's father was an important man in Caithness, so Will escaped punishment. He didn't even have to write lines or get a detention! What's more, when he grew up, he was knighted by the King! The school is still educating boys and it is one of the few in the country with a school rule that says:

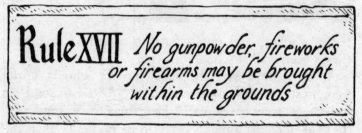

Rule XVII *No gunpowder, fireworks or firearms may be brought within the grounds*

1681 Soon-to-be James VII of Scotland (James II of England), governor in Scotland at the time, passed an act called 'The Test Act' so he could take the throne when his brother, Charles II, died. This act was very unpopular but people who opposed it were hanged. A group of pupils from the George Heriot School in Edinburgh found their own way of opposing the act. They covered a copy of the act in butter and got a dog to eat it … then they hanged the dog. (Sadly the boys were not hanged too.)

1700 A Moffat school teacher was whipped through the streets of Edinburgh and was banished from Scotland for the beating he gave a pupil. He was lucky. The pupil died!

1717 Robert Irvine, a teacher, murdered two boys in his charge. His punishment was to have his hands chopped off before he was hanged. (This made it impossible for him to write on the blackboard, so he wouldn't have been much good as a teacher after that.)

1852 You may think graffiti is a modern problem since spray paint cans are a relatively recent invention. But in this year two boys received 12 lashes each for chalking rude words on a Glaswegian wall.

1870 University students seem to be no better than the school kids. In February this year they carried out snowball attacks on people on Edinburgh's South Bridge. Police were called in and driven back. The students retreated to their university and locked the gates. Police entered from a back gate and defeated the students with truncheons. As the students were led away to jail the public jeered them and started pelting the officers too. The plods then slid into the crowd to make more arrests ... but all they could catch was a little boy.

Cruel Caledonians cwiz

Nowadays school pupils suffer dreaded tests. So why not turn the tables on teacher and see if they can answer these awesome questions…

1 In Caithness, in the reign of Alexander II, 90 people had their feet and hands hacked off. What had they done?
a) stolen the King's cattle
b) boiled a bishop in butter
c) refused to fight against the Viking invaders

2 In 1790 the British navy was forcing men to enlist and fight against the French. Groups of sailors known as the Press Gang snatched men from the streets and taverns. One Scotsman disguised himself as a woman, but they took him anyway. Why?
a) His wife betrayed him to the Press Gang and said, 'Come and get him.'
b) They happened to be looking for women sailors that week. If he'd stayed dressed as a man he'd have been safe.
c) He had a beard.

3 Robert the Bruce's army took the English fort at Kelso while the English held a Pancake Tuesday party. The Scots got close by disguising themselves as what?
a) cows
b) trees
c) women

THIS'LL REALLY CONFUSE 'EM

4 Robert III had an unusual dying wish. What was it?

a) He wanted his ashes blown from a cannon.

b) He wanted his dog to be killed and buried with him.

c) He wanted to be buried in the castle rubbish dump.

5 James, Earl of Douglas, had an unusual funeral. Why?

a) He was so heavy the bearers dropped his coffin and it slid down the steps into the vault, smashing against the family coffins.

b) He was buried face down because he threatened to claw his way out of his coffin to haunt his family.

c) He was the first Scot to be cremated.

6 The present queen, Elizabeth II, is the great (x11) granddaughter of which Scottish ruler?

a) King Macbeth
b) William Wallace
c) Mary Queen of Scots

7 Donibristle Castle was made strong enough to stand attacks from anything, even cannon. But attackers found one weak spot. Where?

a) the dog kennels
b) the gates
c) the toilets

8 What were 'The flowers of Edinburgh'?
a) The thistles that grew through the pavements
b) The smell of the sewage in the street
c) The beautiful Scots women

9 In 1752 a man called Colin Campbell was driving Highlanders out of their cottages. A marksman shot him and escaped. What did the Duke of Argyll do?
a) Hanged somebody else for the crime
b) Arrested the killer's family and threw them in prison
c) Hunted down the killer with trained eagles who clawed him to death

10 One of James III's courtiers protested bitterly about his execution. Why?
a) because he was innocent
b) because he was being hanged with a coarse rope
c) because he'd had to miss his breakfast and he was starving

Answers: **1b)** The bishop was deep fried (without batter) because the people objected to the taxes he wanted to charge them.

2 c) Yes, the sailor had forgotten to shave off his beard!

JINGS! I KNEW THERE WAS SOMETHING I FORGOT TO DO

3 a) The Scottish cow-camouflage worked like a dream. Three hundred years before, King Macbeth had been defeated when his enemy sneaked up behind trees they'd cut down. He must have been suspicious when he saw a forest marching towards him, you'd think.

4 c) Robert was a humble man, with a lot to be humble about. He asked to be buried in the castle rubbish pit with a gravestone that read, 'Here lies the worst of kings and the most miserable of men.'

5 a) Fat James was just too heavy for the coffin bearers. Once they tried to make their way down the stone steps into the underground crypt, the coffin slid off their shoulders. It shot down like a sledge and crashed into his dead relatives. People said this was a sign of doom.

HEY CUT THAT OUT! WE'RE TRYING TO REST IN PEACE DOWN HERE

6 c) Mary Queen of Scots never sat on the English throne but every English and British monarch that came after her was her descendant. She is probably having a good chuckle in her lead-lined coffin at the thought. Scotland rules England, OK?

7 c) The toilets were Donibristle's weakness. Instead of buckets that would have to be emptied, Donibristle Castle had hollow walls – all the toilet waste fell down and out at the bottom. The trouble is, what goes down could come up. The Earl of Huntly lit fires under the toilet holes and the smoke rose up to the top. (Very painful for anyone sitting on the toilet at the time.) The defenders were smoked out and killed.

8 b) Some fussy English travellers said they were unable to sleep for the stink from the Edinburgh streets. Captain Burt wrote, 'I was forced to hide my head between the sheets for the smell of the filth. I was almost poisoned by the stench.' The sewers flowed through the streets while cats, dogs and pigs rooted through the rubbish that was thrown out. On many stairways there was a bucket of waste – and not just waste paper, know what I mean? There was a polluted pond where Princes' Street gardens are now.

9 a) The Duke of Argyll was furious because the people of the village helped the killer to get away. He arrested an innocent man, James Stewart, and made sure he was found guilty, then had him hanged. Argyll's message was clear: 'Let my officers be killed and someone will pay – and I don't care who.'

10 b) Cochrane dressed himself in black velvet and wore gold chains to his execution. It was this flashy dressing and snobbish ways that made him so hated. He argued that a gentleman like him should be hanged with a rope of pure silk not the common sort of rope used for thieves. He was right, of course – I mean, you wouldn't want to be hanged with a rough rope, would you?

Which is witch – the 1600S

James VI of Scotland became king of England and Scotland when Elizabeth I died in 1603. There was no great argument from the English when James headed south to London. Of course he'd had a lot of practice at being a king when he went to England because he'd already ruled Scotland for 35 years. What's more he'd survived!

James brought with him his fear of witches. The Scots were always more worried about this problem than the English. Between 1479 and 1722 over 4,000 men and women were burned as witches in Scotland.

One Scot went to England and made a good living as a witch-finder. He was paid 20 shillings by Newcastle Town Council every time he discovered a witch. With a lot of cheating he 'found' 15 witches there. (Are you surprised?)

The 1600s were going to be just as bloody as the other ages for Scotland.

1600s timeline

1603 James VI of Scotland now rules England as well and wants the two countries to have one government. That is not a popular idea and he has to scrap it. With no English to fight, the Highlanders turn on one another, in a raid called 'the Slaughter of Lennox'.

1605 Guy Fawkes is caught trying to blow up the King and his parliament. But not just because James is a Protestant and the Gunpowder plotters are Catholics. It's also a hatred of the Scots. Guy Fawkes is brought before James and the plotter confesses it had been his hope to blow James and his family 'back to Scotland'.

1612 James's oldest son, Henry Frederick, dies and his second son, Charles, will take the throne. Henry Frederick's death was a bad idea.

1625 James VI dies. An even worse idea because Charles gets his bum on the throne.

1638 Charles I tries to force the Scots to use his prayer book – Scots say 'No' and riot to show they mean it.

1643 Scots and English united ... against King Charles's religious ideas. English parliament goes to war with Charles and Scotland is backing them.

1647 Charles runs away from England after losing the Civil War. He runs home to Scotland. Silly boy. The Scots sell him back to the English.

1649 Charles gets the chop. Now the Scots, who threw out Charles I, support his son, Charles II. (This probably makes sense if you're a Scot.)

1651 Scots crown Charles II as king of England and Scotland (which is a bit cheeky). They then invade England for him ... and are stuffed at Worcester. England's 'Protector' Cromwell, rules Scotland from London. Charles runs away.

1660 Charles II returns as king. 'The killing times' begin when the Scottish religious 'covenanters' rebel and are massacred.

1689 William and Mary take the thrones of England and Scotland and agree that there'll be no bishops in Scotland. Peace all round.

1692 King William makes trouble for the Highland chiefs and their clans – famous Glencoe Massacre this year.

Rough for regents

The crown of Scotland went to the son or daughter of the dying monarch, even if the son or daughter was a child.

Mary Queen of Scots, for example, was just six days old when she became queen. Her son, James VI, was an old man at 13 months when he took over. Most monarchs take the crown and say, 'I promise to rule wisely.' Scottish monarchs probably said, 'Goo-goo-goo-gurgle! Pthththtttt!'

A child is useless as a monarch. They can't do 'grown-up' things like sign execution warrants, squeeze taxes out of peasants or send their loyal subjects out to die in battle. The child needs a guardian – a regent.

Of course this regent has all the power of a king or queen – but the regent has the problem of jealous rivals who fancy this top job. So sometimes it could be rough for regents...

Regent Crighton (died 1454)
Sir William Crighton decided to use his power to get rid of some hated enemies – the Douglas family. James II was just nine

101

years old when Crighton invited two young Douglases to dinner in Edinburgh Castle. Young James greeted them with 'great joy and gladness', it was said. They had a rich feast which ended when Crighton had a bull's head placed on the table in front of the guests. And that was the sign of a death sentence! Crighton took the Douglas boys into the next room, gave them a quick 'trial', before having them beheaded in the courtyard. Young James was upset and probably called Regent Crighton the biggest party-pooper of all time.

Regent Moray (1531–1570)

 James Stewart, Earl of Moray, was unlucky enough to be the stepbrother to Mary Queen of Scots. When she ran off to England he was left in charge of her baby son, King James VI.

He had some letters that seemed to prove Mary had murdered her husband. Mary decided he had to die. First she plotted to have him attacked and murdered in Yorkshire and the letters stolen. Moray heard about the plot and escaped. He rode back to the safety of Scotland – where one of Mary's supporters leaned out of a window and shot him. (What a pane!)

Regents Lennox (1516–1571) and Mar (died 1572)

 The old Earl of Lennox got the job and kept it for a whole year – until he was assassinated in Stirling.

The keeper of Stirling Castle, the Earl of Mar, was the next to take charge of James VI. His reign was even shorter. His death was probably from poison. Who would poison a regent? Maybe someone who wanted to be regent himself. Suspicion falls on the ruthless Earl of Morton...

Regent Morton (1516–1581)

Being regent for James VI is fun. I've brought a new execution machine to Scotland. It's called a guillotine. It's a cut above the rest of the execution methods. And I make a lot of money in this job. If I have to judge a case, then the defendant just has to leave a fat bag of gold on my desk and he'll go free. I set the Laird of Innes free in exchange for all of his lands. The foolish man got drunk, said he'd just like to see me try and take those lands. I sent him to my little guillotine the next day and got the lands all right.

Being regent can be rough. So many enemies! Esme Stewart went to the young King James and said I'd murdered the King's father. I was put on trial and who was sitting on the jury? All my enemies. It's no surprise that I was found guilty. Being a regent they offered me the choice of being hanged or beheaded. I said I wasn't bothered. All my enemies turned out for the execution – Lord Seton took his sons along to watch the sport. I died bravely, of course BUT...

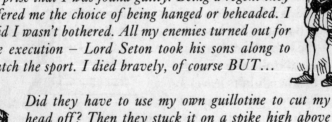

Did they have to use my own guillotine to cut my head off? Then they stuck it on a spike high above the tollbooth in Edinburgh and left it there for 18 months. Nice view, I suppose.

The guillotine that Morton brought to Edinburgh was known as the 'Maiden'. He pinched the idea from the Yorkshire town of Halifax, and Aberdeen pinched it from Edinburgh. The towns near to Edinburgh didn't have to copy the 'Maiden' – they just hired her from Edinburgh. It cost them 30 shillings (£1.50) a go.

103

James VI (1566–1625)

Claim to fame

- Called 'the wisest fool' in the world. He was well-educated but had some simple-minded ideas about things like witchcraft.
- He was a slob. His clothes were old and smelly while his floppy lips meant he spilled as much of his drink as he supped. And he was very fond of drink … very, very fond of it. His nurse had been a drunkard when he was a boy and he learned the habit from her.
- He didn't die a violent death, didn't leave a baby on the throne and didn't ruin the country with endless wars against England. Very unusual for a Scottish King James!

Fantastic fact: In 1590 James sailed to Denmark to collect his 15-year-old bride, Anne. When they reached the mouth of the Firth of Forth, a storm blew up and almost wrecked the ships. He later said the storm was brewed by a coven of witches. He knew this because he saw them, disguised as hares, sailing around his ship in a sieve. When he landed, all the witch suspects in the area were arrested. They blamed his old enemy, the Earl of Bothwell. James and his officers hid in a churchyard to watch a devil-worship ceremony. When they started digging up bodies in the churchyard the officers arrested them – though Bothwell escaped.

LUCKILY I BROUGHT THIS SIEVE WITH ME SO I CAN SAIL ACROSS THE RIVER AND GET AWAY

Funny fact: James I wanted to suck up to Elizabeth I of England. He decided to call his first son Henry after Elizabeth's father. James's wife, Anne, said the child should be called Frederick – after her own father. They agreed that the child should have both names ... but could not agree if he should be Henry Frederick or Frederick Henry. The Bishop of Aberdeen had to christen the child and was too scared to upset either parent. So he said, 'I name this child mumble-mumble-mumble!' James and Anne were both happy because they thought they'd got the name they wanted.

Cruel king: Scotland was never a rich country and James was desperate for the English throne because it would make him rich. As a young man he had borrowed £85,000 from Lord Ruthven ... then had Ruthven executed before he paid it back! Then Ruthven's sons made the mistake of reminding James about the £85,000 he owed them. In no time at all the Ruthven sons were dead! But James was crafty and cruel. He announced that he had been invited to the Ruthven house and rode off. When he got there he locked himself in an upstairs room with his page and a Ruthven son. Suddenly James appeared at the window screaming that the Ruthvens were trying to murder him. By the time James's men got to the room the Ruthvens were dead, stabbed by James's page. Was it a murder plot? Yes – but a plot by James against the Ruthvens, not the other way round.

Foul fact: With the Ruthvens dead, there was no more £85,000 to pay back – dead men don't need money. But James wanted more – he wanted the Ruthven house and lands. He could only have the Ruthven fortune if they were found to be traitors. But they weren't traitors because they hadn't been found guilty. There was only one thing to do; dig up the bodies, take them to court and put them in front of a judge. Not for the first time in Scottish history, this was done.

They were found guilty of treason – and pretty guilty of stinking out the court as they'd been dead for ten weeks. Then, of course, they were hanged, but at least they weren't tortured first. That must have pleased them.

The Bishop's bloodbath

England's Henry VIII showed Scotland how to become Protestants. The Scots really seemed to like the idea and most of them wanted to get rid of all traces of Catholic ceremony from their churches. That meant plain churches with no statues and running their own religion with 'elders' making the rules.

The Protestants didn't like Catholic saints or the bits of saints' bodies that were kept in churches – 'relics'.

These relics were destroyed. To save the saintly Margaret from destruction, the Catholic Abbot of Dunfermline popped her mummified head into a jewelled casket and took it to Mary Queen of Scots, who was a Catholic. What a wonderful present to take to your queen!

The Protestants had one BIG rule.

This bishop business caused a lot of trouble, especially when the English tried to force them to have bishops.

In 1637 the Scots had a riot in St Giles Cathedral, Edinburgh, when Charles I (who was king of England and Scotland) tried to force them to use his prayer book. A woman started it by throwing her stool at the dean when he began reading from it.

A year later the Scots got together and signed an agreement. It was called a covenant and they were known as 'covenanters'.

> Dear Charles
> We are your loyal subjects. But, we don't want your prayer book and we don't want your Bishops.   Signed   The Covenanters

In 1661 the Scottish Protestants (the Presbyterians) sent James Sharp to England to tell Charles II, 'No bishops in Scotland.' What did crafty Charles do? He made James

Sharp into a chief bishop or archbishop, and sent him back to Scotland to sort the Presbyterians out! Archbishop Sharp was not a popular man.

In 1668 James Mitchell tried to assassinate him and Arch-b Sharp made sure he was caught and executed ten years later. Sharp was really, really hated now.

In 1679 Sharp's coach was stopped when nine men hit it with a hail of bullets. They dragged Sharp from his seat and hacked him to death with swords.

Did you know…?

Because the Presbyterians preferred plain churches they often destroyed fine art work in the older churches. 'Art = Catholic', they believed. In 1640, for example, the minister himself, a man called Ross, destroyed the rood screen at Elgin Cathedral.

Wicked witch-hunters

People have been accused of witchcraft for thousands of years – they're even mentioned in the Bible. Witches were tested by dunking in water. A witch was said to be lighter than a normal person. In AD 840 a law was passed that said a witch should be punished by having his or her tongue cut out.

In later years they were taken to the stake and strangled. Strangling was known as 'wirrying'.

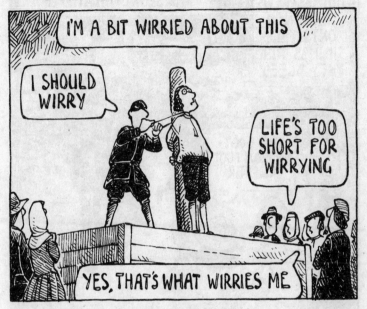

The body was then burned. Of course this was a little bit kinder than being burned alive – but not much. (The kind-hearted English never burned a single witch – but they hanged hundreds of them!)

James the sick sixth

The worst of the witch-hunts were in the 1500s and the 1600s. Sadly and madly, King James VI of Scotland was a great believer in witchcraft. He wrote a very thick (and very stupid) book on the subject.

He was quite sure that people were out to kill him with witchcraft and went along to witch trials to see what went on. Would you get a fair trial with James there? You had more chance of seeing the Loch Ness monster on water skis.

First you'd be tortured. Which would you prefer?

James VI went to the trial of a man accused of witchcraft. First he watched as the man had his fingernails torn out with pliers.

Then James saw the Boot being used on the man. A report says the victim's leg was crushed so badly, 'the blood and marrow spurted out'. Still the man would not confess.

The last witch

The Scottish church court, the presbyter, was very annoyed when King George II of England and Scotland scrapped all the witchcraft laws in 1735. After all, they'd burned their last witch just eight years before and were ready to burn more if they found them.

The later men of the presbyter must have been ashamed of what the witch-hunters had done. In Dundee there is a story that they burned a witch called Grissel Jaffrey – without 'wirrying' her first.

The local legend says...

A young sailor stepped ashore at Dundee and saw a crowd of people round the market cross. He had been born in the town but had been away for many years. When he asked them what was going on they told him that a witch was about to be burned. He decided to stay and watch before going home to see his old parents.

> The fire was lit and the old woman screamed that she was innocent. Through the flames the sailor saw that the victim at the stake was his own mother. He left the town, cursing it and vowing never to return.

Everyone in Dundee believes the story of Grissel Jaffrey, but historians have checked the records of the courts and the church and there is no mention of a witch trial in 1669. The church leaders say the people made it up.

But an old history of Dundee copies a passage from the records of the town council. It says clearly that Grissel Jaffrey was burned after confessing to witchcraft. Not only that but she named other witches in the town.

That history book was written in 1874. The writer saw the record for himself. The record is no longer there. Where has it gone?

Disappeared through witchcraft?

Or removed by people who are ashamed of what the Dundee presbyter did? Which do you think?

Did you know...?

As people learned more from science, they believed less in magic. Scotland has had many great scientists and the boring history books will tell you about the improved steam engine (James Watt), chloroform anaesthetic (James Young Simpson), television (John Logie Baird), the telephone (Alexander Graham Bell), radar (Sir Robert Watson Watt), and so on. But now you can amaze and astonish your teacher by telling them about Doctor Patrick Blair of Dundee. In the 1720s Doc Pat was the first person ever to cut up an elephant to see how its body worked! (It was a circus elephant that died on its way to Dundee.)

Cruel crimes and painful punishments

Crime doesn't pay in Scotland. (After all, Scotland is the home of Doctor Joseph Bell, famous for his clever crime-busting. The author Arthur Conan Doyle turned Joe Bell into a fictional character, the famous detective Sherlock Holmes.)

Stories about crime have always been popular. The trouble is the old stories became changed and it is hard to sort out the fact from the fakes.

Crime cwiz

Here are some horrible historical Scottish stories. Which are (probably) true? And which are (probably) false?

1 Banff, 1700 James McPherson was an armed robber who was brought to trial and sentenced to hang eight days later. The magistrates heard that a messenger was bringing a pardon for McPherson, but they wanted rid of him anyway. So, first they delayed the messenger, then they turned the town clock forward an hour so he was hanged an hour early. He went bravely to his execution playing his fiddle. He then smashed the fiddle over the hangman's head and hanged himself. Because of this cheating the magistrates of Banff lost the power to execute criminals. But is the clock story true or false?

I'M THE MESSENGER. I GOT HERE AT BREAK-NECK SPEED

THAT'S NOT FUNNY

2 Edinburgh, 1688 James Stansfield was found drowned and everyone thought it was an accident. Then it was discovered that his wife had been buying widow's clothes two days before he died! They dug up Stansfield's body

113

and doctors thought they saw strangulation marks on the victim's neck. Servants were tortured so they would tell all they knew, and Stansfield's son, Phillip, was accused. He was then tested. He had to place a hand on the dead body – if the corpse started to bleed then Phillip was guilty. A popular poem of the time tells what happened next...

Young Stansfield touched his father's corpse
Where rose a fearful wail;
For blood gushed through the burial sheet
And every face grew pale.

GUSH

Phillip Stansfield was executed. But is the story true?
3 Galloway, around 1400 Sawney Bean, his children and grandchildren, lived in caves on the wild Galloway coast. They survived by robbing travellers who passed along the coast road. Then, most hideously, they got rid of the evidence by eating the bodies. Human bones were washed up along the shore – but the Beans got away with their gruesome crimes for 25 years! Then a man on horseback managed to fight free of a Bean attack and report them. King James I led troops to the coast and bloodhounds sniffed out the cut-throat clan. They were taken back to Edinburgh and tied to stakes. Their arms and legs were cut off so they bled to death. Gruesome truth or foul falsehood?

THEY'RE NOT ANIMALS, THEY'RE INHUMAN BEANS!

4 Edinburgh, 1828 William Burke and William Hare lived in an Edinburgh slum. They discovered that surgeons needed dead bodies to experiment on. These surgeons were prepared to pay a lot of money for fresh corpses. Burke and Hare became bodysnatchers. They followed a funeral to the graveyard and watched where the coffin was placed. When it grew dark they took shovels and dug it up. They popped the corpse into a sack and carried it off to the hospital. The surgeons paid them well and asked no questions. The two men fell out and Hare turned Burke over to the police who hanged him. Burke and Hare were known as the 'Edinburgh bodysnatchers'. A terrible but true tale?

Answers: **1 False.** There are many legends about McPherson and it is hard to tell which are true. It's said he was part of a gang which planned to rob a house. Then McPherson heard the house owner had just lost his wife and daughter; their bodies were in the house waiting to be buried. Respectful McPherson stopped the gang from going ahead so they betrayed him to the magistrates. The story of him playing his violin on the way to the gallows is unlikely because his hands would be tied. (But a smashed violin can still be seen at the Clan McPherson Museum in Newtonmore.) The truth is that the magistrates sentenced him to hang between two and three o'clock in the afternoon and that's when he died. The clock story is clever, but probably untrue.

2 True. Modern scientists can explain why a corpse might bleed when it is touched ... but modern scientists weren't around in 1688. Phillip Stansfield was hanged, his hand was cut off (for the sin of striking his own father), his tongue was cut out and his head was put on display as an example to others. The story of the bleeding corpse is weird, but probably true.

3 False. The story of the Galloway cannibals is widely believed and repeated in many books. But there is no proof that they ever existed. It is said, for example, that the family was executed without a trial. That is supposed to explain why there were no court records. The truth is the story was first told many years after it was supposed to have happened. It was a good horror story and it was repeated as if it were true. But it isn't. You can go swimming off Galloway beach now with no fear of cannibals – just the fear of freezing to death!

4 False. There were a lot of bodysnatchers in Edinburgh in the 1800s – but Burke and Hare were not bodysnatchers. What they did was find lonely people and offer them a cheap room for the night. When the victim fell asleep, Burke and Hare smothered them and sold the body to the surgeons. They were caught on Hallowe'en night 1828 when their last victim was discovered hidden under a bed. Hare did give evidence against Burke; Burke was hanged and Hare fled to England. He was recognized by angry workmates and blinded. He died a beggar. Burke

> and Hare are the most famous names in bodysnatching history – even though they never dug up a single body. They were simply murderers.

Painful punishments

If the crimes were cruel then the punishments were petrifying. Which of these painful punishments would you like to see in your school ... for teachers, of course!

1402 The Duke of Rothesay was kept prisoner at Falkland Castle in Fife and starved to death. There is a story that he was so hungry he ate his own hands. (Nonsense, of course. He couldn't have held the knife and fork.)

1405 Aberdeen brewers who made bad ale had to pay a 12-pence fine or stand in the pillory. If they did it again then the public could throw eggs, mud and horse-droppings at them. A third offence and they were banished from the town for a year and a day.

1500 Andrew Barton was given the job of keeping the North Sea clear of pirates. To prove he was working hard he sent three barrels to the King, each one full to the brim with pirate heads.

1545 In Stirling, Agnes Henderson was found guilty of insulting another woman. She had to wear a rough hair shirt and walk to church with a candle and beg to be forgiven. As she walked she had to talk to her tongue (difficult), repeating, 'Tongue, you lied!'

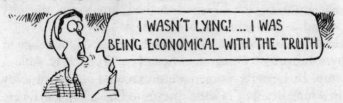

I WASN'T LYING! ... I WAS BEING ECONOMICAL WITH THE TRUTH

1560 Edinburgh Town Council passed a law that said women who nagged their husbands would be punished by the 'branks'. An iron frame was fastened onto the head and a metal spike was forced into the mouth. The woman would be then led through the streets on the end of a chain.

1574 Robert Drummond had left his wife and gone off to live with another woman. He was caught and about to be punished at Mercat Cross in Edinburgh when he pulled out a knife and stabbed himself four times. He died.

1584 A boy set fire to a stack of heather in Edinburgh and caused a panic when people feared the town would burn down. He was caught and was given a roaring fire as a reward. He was burned at the stake.

1585 David Duly, a tailor from Edinburgh, didn't report the death of his wife from the plague. The law officers hanged him outside his own house. But they must have used his own rope, because it snapped. This was seen as a sign from heaven. They banished him from the city instead ... and sent him to Glasgow!

1611 James Watson of Lanark suffered the ancient punishment of being drowned. His crime? He stole a lamb. In Deeside women were executed at this time by drowning in a 'pot'. Cattle thieves in Hawick in 1561 were caught and drowned because there was a shortage of trees and rope!

1640 George Leslie struck his clan chief and the punishment was to have his hand cut off. As the axe was raised the pardon arrived. That was handy.

1685 Two women were put to death by drowning. They were 'covenanters' who refused to accept the rule of the King. All they had to do was say, 'God save the King,' and they'd have lived. They refused and said, 'Glug! Glug! Glug!' instead.

1689 William Mitchell said rude things about the government. He wasn't drowned but simply had his ear nailed to a pillory for an hour.

1700 A Stonehaven thief was sentenced to have both ears burned through with a red-hot iron. As the blacksmith did the burning, one victim cried out, 'I'd be all right now if I had a pair of earrings!'

1709 Elspeth Rule was the last Scot to be tried for witchcraft in the high court. Her punishment was to be banished from Scotland after being burned on the cheek. (Which is better than being burned at the stake.) The key was so hot that witnesses saw smoke coming out of her mouth!

1727 Janet Horne was burned at the stake because she 'helped the devil to put horse shoes on her daughter', to help the lame girl walk.

Horrible hangmen

There were always plenty of people to be hanged in Scotland, so most towns had a full-time hangman. Would you have liked the job?

Here are some of the duties…

Aberdeen, 1578

The town council requires the hangman to *capture* all the *swines* that roam the streets of **Aberdeen**. He will then *execute* the beasts and sell their *meat*. The money shall be handed over to the *council*.

If you didn't fancy giving a porker chops, you could always hang the creature!

Old Aberdeen, 1636

The town hangman shall have the task of rounding up all tramps and beggars in the town and driving them out. The hangman shall then whip any who return or put them in the stocks and brand their cheeks. ~

Archibald Bishop got that job. If any beggar refused to be whipped then the hangman could force any two passersby to help him. If they refused to help with the whipping they were in trouble.

Banff, 1714

The hangman's duties are to include sweeping horse and dog droppings from the streets and to prevent dogs from disturbing church services on a Sunday. He has the power to destroy stray dogs and will be paid 40 pennies for each dog skin he delivers.

You might not have enjoyed collaring collies or gutting greyhounds but Robert Young took the job in 1725. He was in prison at the time, waiting to be hanged. If he refused the hangman's job then he'd have been executed.

Later the Banff job needed someone to punish a young thief by nailing his ear to a stake and burning a mark on his cheek.

When John Reid of Stonehaven was found guilty of stealing linen in 1700, the hangman had to brand him on the shoulder then lead him to the town boundary and kick him on the backside to show he was banned. (A good part-time job for a footballer, maybe.)

On 2 September 1724, Maggie Dickson was hanged in Edinburgh. The doctor signed her death certificate, her body was put on a cart and taken off to the graveyard. On the way Maggie sat up – and scared the life out of the cart driver. The town council decided that they couldn't hang her again since she was officially dead. They let her live and she raised a family before dying naturally 30 years after she was hanged.

> DO YOU BELIEVE IN LIFE AFTER DEATH MAM?

> AYE LAD, AND LIFE AFTER DEATH AFTER LIFE AFTER DEATH

But it was clear that Edinburgh needed a better way to hang people. It was 60 years before they found one and it came about in a curious and horrible historical way...

Drop the dead Deacon

Deacon Brodie was a respected member of the Edinburgh Town Council when they discussed the problem of a crime wave. Someone was robbing the richest citizens of Edinburgh and that someone knew where they kept their money. That someone also had copies of their keys.

'We need to set an example to these villains. We need to hang a few of them in public!' an old councillor cried.

'We do,' the rest of the council muttered.

'But the old gallows need to be replaced,' someone

pointed out.

'And I have an idea for the perfect replacement!' Brodie cut in. 'I am a master carpenter and I've studied the problem. The best way to hang a villain is with the drop!'

'What's wrong with the old system?' someone asked.

'Slow and painful,' Brodie said. 'With my system, the condemned man, woman or child, stands on a trapdoor with a rope round the neck. A bolt is pulled, the trapdoor opens and … Cccct! The end!'

It all sounded very modern and kind to the town council. Brodie was sent away to work on the designs and bring them to the next council meeting.

But at that meeting the council had more urgent matters to discuss than the new scaffold. 'I hear they've arrested a man for these burglaries!' the word was passed around.

'Aye. A man called John Brown. He has not only confessed,' a fat, grinning councillor hissed, 'he has named the man who wormed his way into the rich folk's houses and found their secrets and their keys!'

'Really?' his pinch-faced companion asked. 'What's his name?'

The fat man paused and the yellow-toothed grin filled his face. 'William Brodie!'

'Deacon Brodie? Our own Deacon Brodie!'

'Our very own. They say he had huge gambling debts and turned to robbery to pay for them. All the time he was here and acting like the good citizen. But every night he was creeping into the homes of the rich and robbing them.'

'Well!' the ferret-faced councillor sighed. 'He's sure to hang!'

And he was right. On 1 October 1788, Deacon Brodie stood on the trapdoor of the scaffold and looked down proudly. He turned to the burglar who stood next to him. 'I designed these gallows, did you know?'

'Then you deserve all you get,' the sour-faced burglar snarled.

123

Then the trapdoor opened and Brodie's scaffold was tested for the first time ... on its inventor.[1]

The author Robert Louis Stevenson was fascinated by Brodie's story and the idea of a respectable man turning criminal when night fell. He based his famous book on Brodie, *The Strange Case of Doctor Jekyll and Mr Hyde*.

1. There is a story that Brodie wore an iron collar under his shirt and escaped death. His friends cut him down alive, he was revived and escaped to France. It's a nice story, but very unlikely.

Tartan taming – the 1700s

The Scottish Stuart family ruled England and Scotland in the 1600s. When Queen Anne died in 1714 the government decided to invite the German Protestant Hanover family to rule Great Britain because the Stuarts had gone back to being Catholics.

Most Scots agreed that the German Georges should rule because they hated Catholics even more than the English. But in the Highlands it was different. Many Highland families still liked the Catholic religion and wanted the Stuarts to keep the throne.

The Highlanders, a wild and fearless lot, were prepared to fight and die for the Stuarts – the English were quite happy to let them fight and die. But mainly, die.

The Highlands are a difficult and harsh place to live. The English made it nearly impossible and set about taming the tartan terrors.

Tartan timeline

1696 A new law is passed to set up English schools in the Highlands and 'root out the Gaelic language'. They want the Scots to become Brits. Some hope.

1707 The Scottish parliament votes to abolish itself. Scotland will be ruled from London from now on. It costs just £398,085 to buy off the Scots.

1708 Unhappy Scots rebel and support their King James VIII – but the English call him 'the Pretender'. The Scottish rebels, called Jacobites, lose.

1715 The Jacobites rebel – and lose again.

1745 The Jacobites rebel again, led by the Pretender's son, Bonnie Prince Charlie. They invade England and win battles. Sadly the English people will never support Catholic Charlie so they go home. They are pursued by an avenging Brit army…

1746 The Battle of Culloden. The last battle fought in Britain and one of the bloodiest. Charlie's Highlanders are butchered by the Duke of Cumberland's Brits.

1747 New laws. This time the English aim to break up the system of 'clans' that have been supporting the Jacobites. Anyone caught wearing tartan gets six months in jail. Bagpipes banned for Highlanders. (At least the sheep can get a good night's sleep.)

1763 Ancient Celtic poems by 'Ossian' are discovered. They're probably fakes but the Highlands start to become fashionable. The terrible tourists are about to arrive!

1773 Terrible tourist Dr Johnson arrives from London and writes about smelly Edinburgh and the 'savages' of the Highlands. Still, the English are fascinated.

1782 Highlanders allowed to play the bagpipes and wear tartan again. (36-year-old sheep who remember

them are horrified!)

1787 Glasgow cotton mills are attracting workers from the Highlands. Too many workers. So bosses cut the weavers' wagers. Weavers go on strike. Troops shoot six of them.

1788 In the year that Bonnie Prince Charlie dies, three of King George III's sons in London are fitted out in tartan costumes. The Highlands are getting really trendy in London – while the *real* Highlanders are about to be replaced by sheep!

1792 'The year of the sheep.' Riots by cattle-farmers in Rosshire because their cattle farms are being replaced by the land-owners' sheep. The sheep stay – the cattle farmers start to go.

Horrible Highlands

Scotland is really three countries rolled into one.[1] There are the Borders to the south, the Lowlands in the middle and the Highlands in the north. If Scotland has been battered and beaten in battles it is probably because the three regions haven't been working together.

1. Or four if you count the Orkneys and Shetland which have been affected by contact with countries in Scandinavia.

At Flodden in 1513, it was said the Highlanders liked to have a quick raid, steal some cattle and then go home.

WE WEREN'T PREPARED TO HANG AROUND AND WAIT FOR THE ENGLISH TO MARCH TO THE BORDERS. MIND YOU, THE ONES WHO STAYED AND FOUGHT WITH THEIR DOUBLE HANDED SWORDS WERE DEADLY

Too many Highlanders went home and left King James IV to be defeated.

Meanwhile the Lowland Scots were fighting with pikes – three times the height of a man. A present from their French allies, but useless for a British battle...

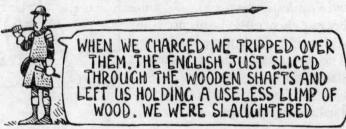

WHEN WE CHARGED WE TRIPPED OVER THEM. THE ENGLISH JUST SLICED THROUGH THE WOODEN SHAFTS AND LEFT US HOLDING A USELESS LUMP OF WOOD. WE WERE SLAUGHTERED

At the same battle the Border soldiers knew the English Border men so well they didn't try very hard to kill them.

MOST OF US HAVE BROTHERS AND SISTERS MARRIED INTO FAMILIES ON THE OTHER SIDE OF THE BORDER. WE WAVED OUR LANCES THEN SET ABOUT OUR REAL BUSINESS–ROBBING THE BODIES ON THE BATTLEFIELD. AND WE DIDN'T CARE IF THEY WERE SCOTTISH OR ENGLISH BODIES

No wonder poor James lost – three regions fighting three different types of battle.

Even their own Scottish king, James VI, said…

As for the Highlanders … the ones that live in the isles are all utterly barbarous.

A Lowland poet showed his disgust of his Highland neighbours in 1560 by writing a poem called, 'How the first Highlander was made by God from a horse dropping in Argyle'.

It's no wonder the English writer, Doctor Johnson, said in 1773…

The people of southern Scotland know as little about the people of the Highlands and islands as they know about Borneo or Sumatra. They have heard a little and guess the rest.

The Glencoe Massacre mystery

King William III in London was always afraid that the Highlanders would rebel – and this was before the famous 1715 and 1745 rebellions happened. He insisted that all the Highland chiefs should swear to be loyal to him. Any chief who failed to take the oath would bring a terrible punishment on his clan. This oath was what lay behind the famous Glencoe Massacre in 1692.

The chief of the MacDonalds in Glencoe went to take the oath but was six days late. This gave William the excuse to rid himself of the MacDonalds. On 1 February 120 troops marched into Glencoe and stayed as guests of the MacDonalds. Two weeks later those troops murdered 38 MacDonald men, women and children. Hundreds escaped, though many died in the blizzards that swept the bleak mountains.

The Highlanders were disgusted – not so much because

of the killings, but because the troops had turned on the people who offered them shelter. That was something a Highlander just doesn't do.

The soldiers…

- shot the elderly chief through the head as he called for wine for them to drink
- shot his wife then bit through her fingers to get her rings off
- clubbed, stabbed or shot the MacDonalds as they lay in their beds
- killed a man ill with fever and his five-year-old son, then threw their bodies in the river
- smeared victims' bodies with dung.

Still, there's a mystery. Some history books have scoffed at the soldiers, saying that they had the simple task of killing 200 unarmed people. They were ordered to kill them all – but they only managed to kill 38! Why?

Maybe the answer is that King William *wanted* them all dead … but many of the soldiers didn't have the heart to do it! Not only did they let 160 escape, but they actually warned the MacDonalds the night before the massacre.

One soldier disobeyed orders by saying to his MacDonald hosts, 'Let's go for a walk.' On the cold mountainside he stopped and started talking to a rock…

The MacDonald hosts took the hint and escaped before the massacre. The story is probably true. The stone, known as Henderson's stone, can be seen in a field at Carnoch near Glencoe.

An eye for an eye and a throat for a throat

The Highlanders were tough because they had a harsh life. Their huts of turf and stone were thatched with heather. Often the only light was what came through the door. It was a single room with a peat fire in the middle – peat is lumps of bog moss, cut into blocks and dried. A pot usually hung over the fire and the smoke made its way out through the roof.

Their clothes were a tartan wool cloth (called a plaid)

131

worn over the shoulder and forming a kilt to the knees. An English visitor, Captain Burt, said...

> *They walk in a stately way for all their poverty.*

But then he complained...

> *Their dress is called a kilt and is so short that if they go up a hill, bend over or are caught in a gust of wind, it is quite disgraceful!*

Captain Burt had quickly found out that these Highland men hadn't discovered underpants. Enemy soldiers discovered that too. The Highlanders liked to fight by charging downhill, swords waving and kilts flying. And not just their kilts, of course. Their naughty bits would be flying too. It must be very hard to fight when you're faced with a sight like that.

The Highlanders were not just fierce fighters. They could be dirty fighters too. There is an amazing story about Ewen, the chieftain of the Camerons, in the 1600s.

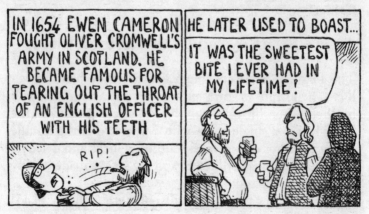

IN 1654 EWEN CAMERON FOUGHT OLIVER CROMWELL'S ARMY IN SCOTLAND. HE BECAME FAMOUS FOR TEARING OUT THE THROAT OF AN ENGLISH OFFICER WITH HIS TEETH

RIP!

HE LATER USED TO BOAST...

IT WAS THE SWEETEST BITE I EVER HAD IN MY LIFETIME!

It was said that Ewen Cameron killed the last wolf in Scotland. He was admired for his toughness.

He once found his son asleep in the hills with a pillow of snow – a tough boy. But Ewen kicked away the snow and told his son that only a softy would use a pillow!

Cruel Culloden

Bonnie Prince Charlie marched into England in 1745 ... and then marched back to Scotland. By April 1746 the English were coming after him. They were led by King George II's son, the Duke of Cumberland, an experienced general known in Scotland as 'the Butcher' ... and not because he sold sausages.

If it had been a boxing match then the referee would have stopped it after one round because it wasn't a fair contest. The odds were against the Scots and a newspaper preview of the fight may have looked like this...

THE SCOT SPECIAL *PULL-OUT* BATTLE SECTION!!

THE CULLODEN CRUNCH

OUR GUIDE FOR THE BIG DAY!!

Charlie's Champs meet the Butcher Boys today at Culloden and some people are saying it will be the decider in this long-running contest. But will it be cheers for Charlie and curtains for Cumberland? Or a Bonnie Prince bloodbath and a battering by the Butcher?

Our experts have been looking at the strengths and weaknesses of the two sides. If you want to get down to the betting shop and make your fortune then here are our top ten tips for today from our reporter on the scene...

	CHARLIE'S CLANS	BUTCHER'S ARMY
NUMBERS	5,000 at the last count. The Frasers and Mackenzies are on their way but our experts say they'll arrive too late. If he waits a day he'll have another 3,500. **Score: 5**	9–10,000 well-trained men. Many of them have fought throughout Europe for years and are well organized. **Score: 10**
STRENGTH	There are no stronger men in the British Isles. But these men have only eaten one biscuit each in the last day or so. A serious handicap. The fighters are awesome men, but there are old men and boys behind them who are quite feeble. **Score: 4**	These men are well-fed and fighting is their career. Yesterday was Cumberland's birthday – he treated them all to bread, cheese and brandy. Still, a ten-mile walk to the battlefield this morning will have tired them. **Score: 6**
TACTICS	The clans prefer sudden attacks from the hills. They are not at their best in an open battle like this. As a result they tried an attack on the Redcoats before dawn. They got lost in the dark and failed. This open ground is good for cannon. Pity the Prince has so few! **Score: 3**	Cannon will mow down hundreds of Scots before they charge. The Redcoats will form into three rows with muskets and simply wait for a Highland charge. When a soldier's shot is fired he still has a bayonet on the end of his gun. **Score: 7**

	CHARLIE'S CLANS	BUTCHER'S ARMY
FITNESS	After that night raid the Clansmen are exhausted and sleeping. The Generals advise the Prince to give them a day's rest. He refuses. Many of the men fell asleep on the wet heather. They are cold, tired and hungry. **Score: 4**	Cumberland knows the Clans are exhausted. He is moving his men forward now so the enemy have no chance to rest. His own men were in bed by ten last night and ready at four a.m. this morning. **Score: 7**
WEAPONS	Many men have lost their shields. They have few cannon and poor horses. The cannon they do have are pointing downhill which makes them difficult to fire. And the gunners aren't very well-trained. **Score: 5**	They have well organized rows of cannon. They'll fire 20 shots to the Highlanders' one. And the bayonet practice has been very useful. The rain is bad news. Keeping the firelocks on their muskets dry. **Score: 7**
COURAGE	The Highlanders would charge at the mouth of a cannon to prove their courage. But their leaders are not so brave. They believe the position is desperate. Even the Prince is losing heart. **Score: 7**	They have a bad record against the clansmen. Faced by a charge they have been forced to flee several times before now. They have a new way of fighting with bayonets that may work against the dreaded Highland charge. **Score: 4**

⚔	CHARLIE'S CLANS	BUTCHER'S ARMY
LOYALTY	The men are united by their hatred for the English, but not much else. Prince Charles has upset many clan leaders because he insists he is the commander. Score: 7	Cumberland has spoken to his men and said that if any were afraid to face the Scots then they could go now and they would not be punished. No one goes. They trust him. Score: 7
LEADERSHIP	Charles is too proud to take advice and too foolish to see the problems for himself. Score: 6	Cumberland is ruthless but his men know he is in charge and are as afraid of him as they are of the enemy. He is fearless in a battle. Score: 8
SPIRIT	Don't forget the Jacobites are defending an unbeaten home record. They are fighting for their lives and their homes as well as their Prince. But this heavy rain seems to be depressing them. Score: 7	They are eager to repay past defeats and to fight against men they see as traitors. They don't think the Scots should be making war when Britain is already at war with France. They are angry and full of vengeance. Score: 6
BATTLEFIELD	Prince Charles refused permission for his officers to check the ground. He doesn't know his men will have to charge through a swamp before they even reach the enemy. Score: 4	This is the sort of battle they are used to. They have time to line up in rows, place their cannon on firm ground and have a clear plan of action. Score: 9
	Total score: 52	Total score: 71

The battle wasn't simply between English and Scots. There were many Scots fighting for Cumberland – they did not like the idea of being ruled by Charlie. The British army followed the bagpipes as well as the clansmen did. There were Irish and English fighting for Charlie.

Cumberland's cannon punched great gaps in the lines of Highlanders and drove Bonnie Prince Charlie off the battlefield. When the Highlanders charged forward they were brilliantly brave and hopelessly lost. It was a massacre and it lasted barely three-quarters of an hour.

Culloden was the last battle to be fought on British soil. It was also one of the most brutal. The Duke of Cumberland gave orders that there should be no prisoners taken. The wounded who were left on the battlefield were murdered. There are even stories of Highland prisoners being burned alive.

But the really tragic thing was that it was the start of the government's campaign to clear out these Highland Scot troublemakers once and for all. It was the end of the Jacobite rebellions and the start of the 'clearances'.

Life in the old Highlands had been hard – the British government in London decided to make it impossible.

Ten things you don't want to know about Prince Charles

(No, not the *modern* Prince Charles, you dummy. The Prince Charles Edward Stuart – known as Bonnie Prince Charlie.)

This man was a loser, yet went on to become one of Scotland's greatest heroes. If you want to be a hero then take a tip from Charlie…

1 Charlie's father, James, was born in England, his mother, Clementina, was Polish and Charlie himself was born in Rome. Charlie spent most of his life in France. He may have claimed the Scottish throne for his father, but he didn't know a dirk from a kirk.

2 When he landed at Eriskay Island on 23 July 1745, he had only seven supporters yet he planned to conquer Britain. Heroic act number one: star of 'The Magnificent Seven'.

3 He sheltered in a fisherman's hut and nearly choked on the smoke. The young prince wasn't used to this tough Scottish life. He met the clan chieftain the next day, and the Scots lord who thought Charlie's idea of winning the throne was plain daft. He said, 'Go home.' Charlie said, 'I *have* come home.' (This wasn't exactly true, but it was a brilliantly clever thing to say, you have to admit.)

4 Charlie led his 5,000 clansmen into England. Surprise, surprise, the English didn't want his dad, James, to be king. So he turned round and marched back to Scotland. Even bigger surprise! A lot of the Lowland Scots didn't want a Stuart king again. The Bonnie Prince was upset.

5 He was even more upset when the chieftains said the little army should go back to the safety of the Highlands, even though they had beaten the British forces every time they'd met them. 'Good God!' Charlie pouted. 'Have I lived to see this?' He thought it couldn't get worse. At Culloden it did.

6 Charlie said, 'I have made a firm promise that I will conquer or die! I shall stand my ground as long as I have a man remaining with me!' Another great speech – and another heroic pose. He'd have been a great manager of a Scottish rugby team ... but a poor player. He didn't conquer or die or stand his ground. He ran away after Culloden, yet that's when the hero stuff *really* starts.

7 Life on the run, hunted by some savage Brits, was as dangerous, adventurous and exciting as an Enid Blyton book! You know the sort of thing, sailing through storm-lashed seas, stepping out of a cave hiding-place to see the King's ships searching for him. Of course Enid's heroes don't keep warm by drinking a bottle of brandy a day. Charlie did, and it was *not* a healthy, heroic thing to do (so we won't mention it).

8 From an Enid Blyton adventure he stepped into a mushy romantic novel. He met the brave Highland lassie, Flora MacDonald. She risked her young life to take him across to a safe hiding-place on the Isle of Skye. He dressed up in petticoats as her maid-servant, Betty Burke, and as they crossed the sea he sang Flora to sleep. (It's so

romantic it could make a Horrible Histories reader want
to throw up, couldn't it?)

9 As the Redcoat net closed in, Charlie dressed in a kilt and
an old shirt. He slipped through the net by crossing the
heather-covered hills, barefoot, through sleet and rain.
When news came of a French ship off the coast he hopped
onto it and went back home. (Oops! Sorry. He *was* home,
wasn't he?) He went back after one-and-a-half glorious
years of Scottish adventure. He never returned to Scotland.
10 Charlie's big mistake was to live another 40 years. The
best heroes die young – Charlie died a bad-tempered
drunkard, pathetic and pickled like an onion with all that
brandy. The country and the people he left behind are
still suffering after over 200 years. Loyal Jacobites still
remember him as a 'Bonnie Prince' – horrible historians
remember him as a 'Charlie'.

Cut-throat clearances

The Highlanders had been defeated at Culloden. Now
the British government had to make sure those kilted
killers never clasped a claymore again.

The 'clearances' were about to begin.

First the Duke of Cumberland's Redcoats hunted
down the clansmen who had escaped from Culloden.
Prisoners were treated so badly that they died in their
hundreds. The survivors were sent to the American

plantations as slave labour. Clans that had supported Bonnie Prince Charlie had their houses burned to the ground and their cattle driven off.

Then the British government passed laws...

THE DISARMING ACT 1746

LET IT BE KNOWN THAT IT IS AGAINST HIS MAJESTY'S LAWS TO:

Carry weapons
Wear tartan
Wear the kilt
The bagpipes are banned as
an instrument of war

Punishments:
First offence-six months imprisonment
Second offence-transportation to any of
His Majesty's plantations for seven years

In fact, King George's soldiers were ordered to go further; if they saw any man in tartan then they must kill him on the spot.

Even in the Lowlands a woman was arrested for wearing a dress with a tartan pattern.

The Disarming Act was withdrawn 36 years later, but by then the clan system was falling apart and the weavers had lost the art of tartan weaving. Thirty years later tartans were collected and 'The Highland Society' tried to sort out the confusion of which tartans belonged to which families. And they're still trying!

The truth is that Highlanders wore whatever the local weaver made. If a clan all went to the same weaver then that clan all wore the same tartan.

Since the 1820s hundreds of new tartans have been produced. Even some football teams have their own tartan. (No, the players don't run around in kilts.)

The clan system

The clans were large families – 'clan' is from the Gaelic word for 'children'.

I AM THE CLAN CHIEFTAIN. I PROTECT MY PEOPLE IN TIME OF FAMINE AND HARDSHIP

IN RETURN, WE CLANSMEN FIGHT IN HIS PRIVATE ARMY IN TIMES OF WAR

AND I LOOK AFTER THE FARM WHILE THEY GO BASHING EACH OTHER WITH CLAYMORES

WE USE THE 'RUNRIG' SYSTEM. EVERYONE HAS A STRIP OF LAND TO GROW OATS AND BARLEY AND HAVE A FEW BLACK CATTLE

AND IN THE SUMMER WE TAKE CATTLE UP TO THE HILL AND LIVE IN STONE HUTS WE CALL SHIELINGS

The years of the sheep

The runrig system produced enough food for a clan to live on – usually. But down in England, they discovered there was a better way to organize things – get rid of the strips of land. Join them all together to make large fields, then fill the fields with sheep, sell the wool and mutton and make *money*.

What could the clansmen and their families do when the Lowland shepherds and their flocks of Cheviot sheep moved in?

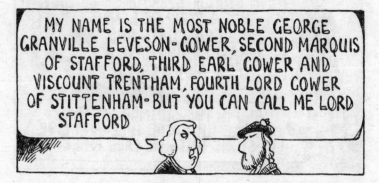

Of course many went south to the towns – Glasgow grew from 12,000 people in 1710 to 200,000 120 years later. If Lord Stafford thought the Highland huts were bad then he should have seen the Glasgow slums!

In 1792 there was a small rebellion when 400 Highlanders drove about 6,000 sheep south. (Even though they were poor and hungry they didn't kill a single sheep for food.)

A few of the men were caught and imprisoned. Before they could come to trial they slipped out of a jail door that someone had left open and no one was ever punished.

The people who didn't want to leave were forced out by soldiers. The men who did Lord Stafford's dirty work were called 'factors', and the most hated was the dreaded Patrick Sellar.

Suffering Sellar

Patrick Sellar helped Lord and Lady Stafford to clear the Highlanders off the land and turn it into sheep farms. Lady Stafford called him 'exceedingly greedy and harsh'. He was especially keen to get the farmers off land at Rossal because he had rented it to put sheep on it himself.

That's when he was accused of murder. Here are some witness statements…

My name is Angus Mackay. I was asleep in the house when Sellar's men arrived to burn down our house. I took my young brother on my back and ran down to the river. It was so cold and deep he was crying and shaking on my back. I fell and couldn't rise. We were both crying and terrified that we would drown. A poor woman was coming up the path with her family, she saw us, jumped in the river and swept us out.

But it was the old and the sick who suffered even more…

My name is William Chisholm. My mother, who was almost 100 years old, was in the house when Sellar came and told us to move. I said she was too sick to travel. Sellar said, 'Damn the old witch. She has lived too long. Let her burn'.

The house was set on fire and my mothers blankets were set on fire as we were getting her out. We put her in a shed and it was all we could do to stop them burning that too! She died within five days. Sellar killed her.

There were other injuries among the 27 families who were cleared out…

My name is John Mackay. My wife is expecting a baby and did not want to move. She climbed onto the roof to stop them setting fire to our house. She fell through the roof and was

> badly hurt. Old Donald Macbeth was dying of skin cancer yet they cleared him from his cottage. He was left lying in the open for days with no other home to go to.

Patrick Sellar's defence was…

> I was only doing my job. We had given these people homes on the coast where they could farm and fish.

In fact the new land was too poor to farm. They were forced to make shelters from earth walls with blankets stretched over the top. Wood was difficult to find in Sutherland, yet Sellar did not allow them to take the wood from their old homes with them. And they were given no money to build new homes.

Some historians think Sellar was a fair man and say the Highlanders are too harsh on him.

If you had been the judge, what would you have said? Guilty … or not guilty?

Answer: Patrick Sellar was found 'not guilty' and allowed to go on to become one of the richest sheep farmers in the region.

Thirty years later, a bitter poet wrote about Sellar's clearances and it is this bitterness that is remembered…

Lady Stafford, what's become
Of your soft, lovely silken dress?
Does it protect you from grave worms
That eat their way inside your flesh?

Loathsome Sellar, in your grave,
Have you the pay you earned so well?
The fire you used to burn the thatch,
Does it now burn your beard in Hell?

Patrick Sellar is buried in the ruined Elgin Cathedral. An old caretaker says that visitors from Canada and the United States asked to be shown his grave. They were the descendants of the Highlanders that Sellar drove out of Scotland.

When these visitors were shown the grave they spat on it – perhaps they still do. And they don't do it to put out the fire in his beard.

Did you know…?
If you wanted to escape the clearances and get to Canada or the US, you could buy a place on a ship for 30 shillings (£1.50). But for that amount you got just 0.28 square metres – measure it and see if you can fit! It's no wonder that disease spread through the packed Highland families. In 1826 the ship *James* landed in Canada and every single person on board suffered from the deadly disease typhus.

Weird words

Blame Thomas the Rhymer. He was one of the great early Scottish poets. But it wasn't so much his poetry that made him famous, it was his ability to foresee the future.

He told King Alexander III not to have his wedding in Kelso Abbey in 1285 or the roof would fall in on the congregation. The wedding was moved to Jedburgh Abbey instead. And would you believe it? Yes, the roof of Kelso Abbey fell down!

Amazing? Well, not exactly. It was another 500 years before the roof fell down and Alexander was dead anyway, as you might expect.

But Thomas did see skeletons dancing at Alexander's wedding – no one else saw them, of course – and Alexander died five months later. (Five months is better forecasting than 500 years, you have to admit.)

McGonagall's masterpieces

Some of the best writers in the world have been Scottish – if you ever have a spare year then read Sir Walter Scott's books. Magic.

Sadly, some of the worst writers in the world are also Scots. Take William McGonagal (1825–1902), for example. A sad and tragic man. Everybody tried to tell him he was the world's worst poet but he didn't believe them!

McGonagall thought people were too stupid to see what a great poet he really was. Here is his sad life story…

   William Topaz McGonagall was a Dundee weaver who gave up his work to become a travelling poet. He performed in public houses but was unpopular because his poems spoke of the evils of drink…

Strong drink makes the people commit all sorts of evil,
And must have been made by the Devil.
For to make them quarrel, steal and fight,
And prevent them from doing right.

It's not surprising that landlords drove McGonagall out of their bars by pouring stale beer over his head. They would hide his hat and leave it cut to pieces. That's fair enough considering the way he cut the English language to pieces…

Then, all ye tourists, be advised by me,
Beautiful Edinburgh ye ought to go and see.
It's the only city I know of where you can wile away
*   the time,*
By viewing its lovely scenery and statues fine.

McGonagall performed anywhere he could find an audience: church halls, blacksmith shops, a circus and even in schools to poor trapped children. It must have been worse than a maths lesson, because McGonagall was especially fond of 'disaster' poems, like the tragedy in a Sunderland theatre where 200 children died in a crush…

> The innocent children were buried seven or eight
>   layers deep,
> The sigh was heart-rending and enough to make one
>   weep;
> It was a most affecting spectacle and frightful to
>   behold,
> The corpse of a little boy not above four years old.

The council of Dundee tried to stop McGonagall touring because they said he gave the city a bad name! His wife had to work in a laundry to scrape a living; she begged him to go back to weaving. People laughed at him in the street and threw stones at him. Still he went on. He wrote two poems to the Tay Railway Bridge, saying how fine and strong it was. When it blew down he wasn't too upset. He was able to write a poem about the disaster…

> *Beautiful railway bridge of the silvery Tay*
> *Alas! I am very sorry to say*
> *That 90 lives have been taken away*
> *On the last sabbath day of 1859*
> *Which will be remembered for a very long time.*

McGonagall was like the Tay Railway Bridge -- a disaster who 'will be remembered for a very long time' ... for all the wrong reasons.

Did you know...?
When the Tay Bridge collapsed, a train fell into the river and many passengers were drowned. (The English said it served them right for being wicked enough to travel on a Sunday!) The locomotive from the train was hauled out and repaired. The sick Scottish railwaymen nicknamed it 'The Diver'. And, talking of bridges...

The famous Forth Bridge was opened in 1890 by the Prince of Wales (because there wasn't a Prince of Scotland). He hammered in rivet number 7,000,000 (but didn't help with the other 6,999,999). Fifty-seven men died building it, but no one has been reported dying of laughter at the horrible historical joke...

Pop poet

Scotland's favourite poet is Robert Burns. He came from a humble home but his talent made him a national hero. Here are five curious facts about Burns...

1 Robert Burns's father was William Burnes. Maybe he couldn't spell! And his mother was Agnes Broun so it looks like her spelling was even worse! Today their gravestone spells their names 'Burns' and 'Brown'. But that's their third gravestone. The first two were chipped to pieces by fans of Robert Burns who wanted souvenirs of his family.

2 Mrs Burnes had an old maid who told Robert tales when he was a child. Robert later said, 'She had the largest collection in the county of tales and songs concerning devils, ghosts, fairies, brownies, witches, warlocks, kelpies, elf-candles, wraiths, giants, enchanted towers, dragons and other nonsense. From this grew the seeds of my poetry.'

3 Robbie started travelling around Scotland collecting old songs and having them published before they were forgotten. But he cheated a bit because he changed them and added verses when he thought the songs needed them. It's impossible to tell, now, what bits are old Scottish and what bits were Robbie's invention. Sometimes he took an old tune and added words where there had never been words before. The most famous song is *Auld Lang Syne* that people sing at New Year. He said that it was an old song but he probably did write most of it.

4 Burns was never very rich. 'I'll be damned if I ever write for money,' he said. His farm was on poor ground and never made money. He took a job as an officer with the customs service, trying to stop smugglers. In July 1796 he wrote to his publisher and begged, 'I implore you for five pounds. I owe the money to a cruel scoundrel of a shopkeeper who has taken it into his head that I am dying. Do, for God's sake, send me that sum. The horrors of jail have made me half-mad.'

5 In fact, the shopkeeper was right. The poet was very ill. He'd had a few drinks with friends and set off to walk home. He fell asleep on the roadside before he made it home and this probably gave him rheumatic fever. Robbie Burns died two weeks after his plea for five pounds. He was just 36 years old.

Weird words

Robbie Burns wrote the way Scottish people spoke. That's not always so easy for English-speakers to understand. For example, the word 'sic' means 'so'. When a Scot says 'I'm sic sick,' it doesn't mean they want to throw up twice.

You may need a quick course in the weird words that the Scots use. (If you are a Scottish reader then you may want to skip this section.)

Not many people know that Goldilocks was a Scot – why do you think she was so desperate to get a bowl of porridge? And, as you already know from this book, there used to be bears in Scotland. So here it is, the story of the Three Bears, the way it was meant to be told...

The carfuffle Goldilocks caused when she plunked

Ane forenoon yon three bears decided tae gang forth frae their bothy for a dander. The heid bummer was Faither McBear, wha was a crabbit auld carnaptious craitur. The wifie was Mrs McBear, a douce and canny body. The wean was Malcolm McBear, a peelie-wally bairn who was always girnin. 'Maun we gan?' wee Malcolm speired.

'Wheest and haud yer mou or aa'l skelp yer lug, yer glaikit chiel,' Faither McBear said.

Sae, aff they went, forgetting tae drap the sneck on the door.

Intae the woods cam Goldilocks, a gallus, shilpit besom who was plunking off school. But noo she was wabbit wi stravaigin roon the forest. She cam tae the McBear but-and-ben, lifted the snib and caad, 'Parritch! A maun hae parritch!'

She picked up the spurtle and tried Faither McBear's dish. 'Och!' she hoasted. 'Ma thrapple! Tae het!'

Then she tried Mither McBear's parritch. 'Like glabber! Tae wersh an' caud!'

Last she tried Malcom McBear's parritch. 'No bad!' she said and pushed ilk drap in her muckle mou.

Whit a stramash when the three McBears got hame! Whit a rammy! 'Fegs!' Faither McBear ca'd. He was gey fashed.

Mither McBear cried, 'Wae, wae, wae!' She was aal shoogly.

Puir wee Malcolm McBear cried, 'Wheer's ma parritch? There's nane!'

The feartie Goldilocks had rin awa doon the clarty causey, intae the forest.

'Whit wa ganna dae?' Faither McBear speired.

'Aa dinna ken,' Malcolm said.

'Ye'll just hae tae eat haggis,' Mither McBear said.

Dire dictionary

For the really boring reader who actually wants to understand the above drivel, or talk like a Scot, here's a quick dictionary:

Dictionary

aff: off
ane: one
auld: old
bairn: child
besom: nasty woman/girl
bothy: rough turf cottage
but-and-ben: two-room cottage
cam: came
canny: pleasant
carnaptious: bad-tempered
causey: path
chiel: child
clarty: muddy
crabbit: bad-tempered
craitur: creature
dander: stroll
dinna: don't
douce: sweet-natured
fashed: upset
feartie: cowardly
feg: I'm annoyed!
forenoon: morning
forth: out
frae: from
gallus: cheeky
gang: go
gey: very
ganna: going to
giming: whingeing
glabber: soft, sticky mud
glaikit: stupid (very)

haud: hold
heid bummer: boss
hoasted: coughed
ilk: each or every
lug: ear
maun: must
mou: mouth
muckle: big
noo: now
och: Oh, I say!
parritch: porridge
peelie-wally: wimpy
plunking: skiving
rummy: a noisy disturbance
sae: so
shilpit: skinny
shoogly: shaky
skelp: slap
sneck/snib: door catch
speired: asked
spurtle: wooden porridge stirrer
stavaiging: wandering
stramash: fuss
tae: to
thrapple: throat
wabbit: worn out
wean: small one (child)
wersh: tasteless
wha: who
wheest: shut up!
whit: what

No wonder the English gave up trying to conquer the Scots.

Scottish sense

The Scots are very sensible.

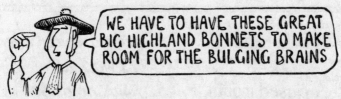

WE HAVE TO HAVE THESE GREAT BIG HIGHLAND BONNETS TO MAKE ROOM FOR THE BULGING BRAINS

This wisdom is passed down in the wit and wisdom of Scottish proverbs. Who can argue with the sense of saying...

A bit but and a bit ben, maks a mim maiden at the board end.

Who can argue with that? Who can even *understand* it? Some of the sayings are quite clever, once you understand them. Impress your teacher with your wisdom by repeating the old Scottish proverb...

Everything has an end – but a pudding has two.

Others are simply weird...

Eagles catch no fleas.

OK THEN ....

159

That's *true* ... but a peculiar thing to say. Eagles catch rabbits and rats but not fleas. I guess the little fleas just keep slipping out of those huge claws.

Now that you understand the Scottish proverb-writer's brain you should have no trouble matching up these sayings.

1 A bald head... *a... gets no whiter when it's washed*

2 A closed mouth... *b... holds no poison*

3 A crow... *c... is easily shaved*

4 A hungry stomach... *d... needs a lot of cleaning*

5 A blind man... *e... catches no flies*

6 An old pot... *f... won't howl if it's knocked over by a bone*

7 A green turf... *g... has no need of a mirror*

8 A dog... *h... is a good mother-in-law*

9 A scabby sheep... *i... has no ears*

10 A horn spoon... *j... often infects a flock*

The above sayings make a lot of sense, if you think about them. Almost as much sense as the real proverbs. It's a shame to unscramble them, but here goes...

Answers: **1 c)** A bald head … is easily shaved. Meaning: An easy job is soon finished. (So do your homework now and stop reading this book.)

ON THE OTHER HAND…

2 e) A closed mouth … catches no flies. Meaning: Keep quiet and keep out of trouble. (So don't answer back when teacher tells you to clean the blackboard.)

3a) A crow … gets no whiter when it's washed. Meaning: People never change. (So it's no use expecting a mean old crow like your dad to increase your pocket money.)

HOW ABOUT TOILET BLEACH?

4 i) A hungry stomach … has no ears. Meaning: A hungry person is an angry person who won't listen to sense. (So don't argue when the school bully jumps the queue for school dinners.)

AHHHHHHH!

I TRIED TO WARN HIM BUT HE WAS TOO HUNGRY

5 g) A blind man … has no need of a mirror. Meaning: Your appearance is not all that important. (So you don't have to spend all day looking at yourself, big head.)

6 d) An old pot ... needs a lot of cleaning. Meaning: Old things are cheap to buy but expensive to keep. (So tell your mum to buy you those new trainers for £250.)

7 h) A green turf ... is a good mother-in-law. Meaning: A grave (covered in turf) is the best place for a mother-in-law. (This is cruel and untrue – and likely to get your dad a thick ear if he repeats it.)

8 f) A dog ... won't howl if it's knocked over by a bone. Meaning: You don't hurt people by throwing things at them they'll enjoy. (This is not a wise proverb to repeat if you enjoy pianos.)

9 j) A scabby sheep ... often infects a flock. Meaning: One bad person in a group turns the whole lot bad. (So you can blame the worst person in your class for your rotten school report! Useful!)

10 b) A horn spoon ... holds no poison. Meaning: Having a meal in a poor house (with spoons made of horn) is better than a fine meal in a rich house. Poisoners kill for money in the rich houses. (So if you haven't got a horn spoon you'd better eat your soup with a fork, to be on the safe side.)

Now you have the wit and wisdom of Scotland in your head ... though, personally, I prefer to remember that bald heads get no whiter when they're washed, and old pots won't howl if they're knocked over by a bone.

Great gravestones

The deaths of kings are recorded by writers for history. But the only clue to the deaths of common people are from their gravestones. Here are five of the funniest...

1 In a Sutherland Churchyard...

Here doth lie the body
Of John Flye
Who did die
By a stroke from a sky-rocket,
Which hit him in the eye-socket.

A painful reminder that fireworks should always be handled by sensible children and not stupid adults.

2 Still, there are worse ways to die. Take poor Roger Norton's epitaph from his tombstone at Greenock...

Here lies, alas, poor Roger Norton,
Whose sudden death was oddly brought on!
Trying one day his corns to mow off,
The razor slipped and cut his toe off!
The toe (or rather what it grew to)
The part then took to mortifying[1]
Which was the cause of Roger's dying.

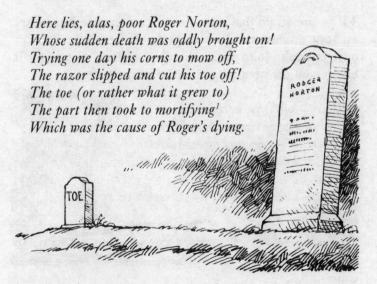

---

1. It turned poisonous.

3 You'll notice it's easy to write an epitaph if your name is easy to rhyme – 'Flye' and 'die' were made for each other. 'Norton' and 'brought on' was a little trickier. But some writers get a bit carried away with the rhyming … they just can't stop!

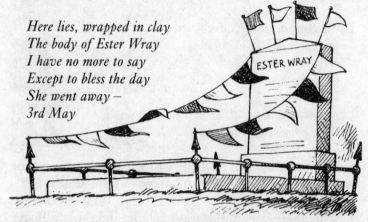

Here lies, wrapped in clay
The body of Ester Wray
I have no more to say
Except to bless the day
She went away –
3rd May

Ester's husband was obviously glad to be rid of her.

4 If you're afraid that someone will write something nasty on your gravestone then it's probably best to write your own epitaph. John Gray did this. (Quick tip: write it before you die because it's hard writing it after.)

Poor John Gray, here he lies,
Nobody laughs and nobody cries;
Where he's gone, and how he fares,
No one knows and no one cares.

Sad.

5 Some graves have messages that give you a lot to think about. A glover, John Geddes, is buried at Elgin with this message for you…

> *If life were a thing*
> *That money could buy,*
> *The poor could not live*
> *And the rich would not die.*

English epic

The English wrote *God Save the King* as a hymn. It was really a prayer to protect the King, against the 1745 rebels from Scotland. Then General Wade built wide roads to help move English armies into the Highlands and crush the Highlanders. The English were so grateful to Wade they added another verse to the national anthem. If you think McGonagall's verse is bad you should see the verse the English poet added. (Try singing it to the tune of *God Save the Queen*.)

> *God grant that General Wade*
> *May by thy mighty aid*
> *Victory bring.*
> *May he sedition hush,*
> *And like a torrent rush*
> *Rebellious Scots to crush,*
> *God save the King!*

The roads also helped the Jacobite armies to invade England! In Fort William someone pinned up a poem that read...

If you'd seen these roads before they were made,
You'd hold up your hands and bless General Wade!

Happy history – modern Scotland

Wally the wizard

Scottish history before 1820 was truly horrible at times, and miserable and sad at times. People remembered the misery and forgot some of the glorious things that had been done. In 1820 Scotland was settling down to become 'North Britain'.

'Caledonia' and 'Pictland' had vanished from the memories of most people. In another hundred years the name 'Scotland' could have gone the same way.

Then along came a Scot called Scott! He was the most popular writer of his age – Sir Walter Scott (1771–1832). He invented Scottish history all over again.

Sir Walter started writing historical novels. And these novels were based on Scotland's past.

Scott made that past sound like a glorious and glamorous time to live. Scotsmen and Scotswomen were heroes and heroines...

- Scott wrote about the heroic deeds of Rob Roy. Rob Roy MacGregor became a sort of Scottish Robin Hood when he was really a cattle-thief and outlaw.

- The Scottish crown jewels had been locked away for 111 years since Scotland became part of Great Britain. Scott had them brought out for the world to see the glory of Scotland's past.

● Scott organized a two-week visit of King George IV to Scotland. The King was met by chieftains and clansmen in new tartan. Fat George even wrapped a huge kilt around himself and was cheered as 'the chief of chiefs'. (Fat George didn't want to risk a gust of wind lifting his kilt and showing his naughty bits to the Scots. He wore pink tights under the kilt.)

PINK TIGHTS AND TARTAN? PINK TIGHTS AND TUTU? IT'S SO CONFUSING

The Lowland tradesmen cashed in by selling miles of tartan to Scots and English who had never seen a glen or a ben.

What were the real Highlanders doing while George was being cheered in Edinburgh? Being driven out of the Highlands, heading for the Lowland towns or emigrating to America to try and survive, that's what.

Lowlanders were happily singing a song written for Bonnie Prince Charlie, *Will ye no' come back again?*. Of course they didn't *really* want him to come back! (The Lowlanders never wanted him when he was there in the *first* place and they had their chance!) Anyway, he'd been dead 30 years by the time this song was being sung. He'd have been a bit mouldy if he had come back!

Even the Highlands themselves became part of the magical New Scotland idea. They used to be a cold, bleak wilderness. Now they were wonderful, rugged and unspoilt scenery. (This is plain daft! You can't even see any scenery because these ugly lumps of mountains get in the way!)

Before Sir Walter Scott ... miserable, cold, bleak wilderness

So, next time you join the tourist trail to Scotland and can't see the scenery because the roads are jammed with cars and caravans, remember ... blame Walter Scott.

After Sir Walter Scott ... wonderful, rugged, unspoilt scenery

Nasty 19th century

So Sir Walter Scott had invented a new 'history' of Scotland where everyone was a hero – a cattle-thief like Rob Roy, a killer queen like Mary Queen of Scots and a pathetic prince like Charlie.

But the real Scotland of the 1800s wasn't a happy land of little farmers (known as crofters) shearing their sheep or feeding their cattle or milking their bagpipes. Many of the Scots were moving to the towns to find work. Of course the towns grew bigger and more crowded and more dirty and more deadly. An 1842 government report said…

> Glasgow is possibly the filthiest and unhealthiest of all British towns. The passageways that link the tenements are little more than open sewers. It is no surprise that half of the children die before the age of five.
>
> *Edwin Chadwick*

The snobs of Edinburgh complained they couldn't understand the Highlanders because they spoke Gaelic. But they were happy enough to let the Highlanders labour on, building a fine new town centre for them. The poor were left to crowd into the old town centre till it turned into slums. Chadwick said…

> Edinburgh is not much better than Glasgow with its filthy, overcrowded, one-roomed dwellings.

The hefty Highland men also took over the city's sedan chair business – carrying people around the new town in chairs.

But it was in the industrial towns where life was hardest…

Wicked work

The Flying Scot

YESTERDAY'S BINGO NUMBERS INSIDE !!!! | *1 September 1820*

CHOP! WEAVER WILSON PAYS PRICE

James Wilson, the 60-year old rebel leader, was brutally executed yesterday. The weavers' leader was fastened to a wooden sledge and dragged to a scaffold in front of the law courts in Glasgow. The old man wore an open-fronted shirt over his white prison uniform and white gloves. His mysterious travelling companion wore a black mask and carried an axe.

Last week Wilson was found guilty of treason. In April he had marched from the Lanarkshire village of Strathaven at the head of a small group of rebels. Wilson was armed with a rusty old sword and his followers had poor weapons. When they arrived in Glasgow they found the city was quiet and there was no support. They were easily arrested and brought to trial.

The judge sentenced him to suffer the ancient form of execution like William Wallace, to be hanged, drawn and quartered. A crowd of 20,000 gathered to watch the gruesome spectacle and there was a large guard of dragoon soldiers to prevent trouble.

Wilson was hanged and

Rebel head Wilson

died bravely. He was then cut down and beheaded with a single stroke of the axe. The executioner held up the white-haired head and cried, 'Behold the head of a traitor,' as was the old custom. The crowd jeered and hissed in disgust, crying, 'Shame!' and 'Murder!'

Some of the soldiers fainted at the sight. It was decided to spare his corpse the disgrace of being cut into quarters. He was thrown into a pauper's grave in Glasgow but his niece had the body dug up and returned to the church-yard in his Strathaven home.

Wilson's supporters have been distributing handbills telling his true sad story and saying, 'May the ghost of the murdered Wilson haunt the pillow of his cruel judge.'

Next week the rebels Baird and Hardy will go to a similar death in Stirling. Isn't it time Scotland gave up this barbaric punishment? No man deserves to die the way Wilson died. The judge called him a 'miserable and sinful creature'. Many poor Scots will see him as a martyr for a free Scotland.

BUT THE 1837 STRIKE FAILED AND THE LEADERS WERE TRANSPORTED FOR SEVEN YEARS

IT'S BETTER THAN LOSING YOUR HEAD. IT'S BACK TO WORK I SUPPOSE

Horrible housing

When Highlanders moved south to work in towns like Glasgow they needed somewhere to live. They were packed into the cheapest and gloomiest slum houses possible. So Victorian housing officers began 'ticketing' houses – police would raid them in the middle of the night to check that they weren't overcrowded.

By the end of the 1800s the slums were being knocked down and replaced by 'tenements' – flats.

The trouble was, the standard of tenements varied. In Dundee in 1905 it depended which side of the road you lived on...

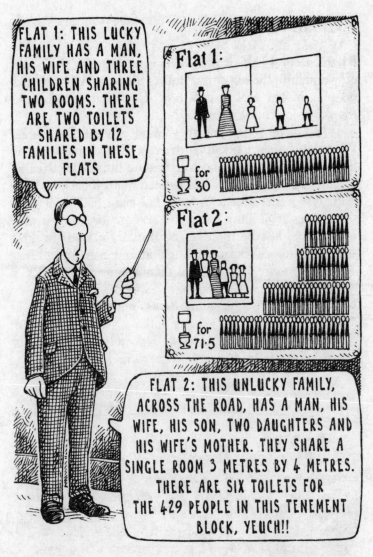

Two flushing toilets for 12 families may not sound like much, but in Dundee, 40 years before, there were just *five* flushing toilets for the *whole* city of 92,000 people … and three of those were in hotels. (Imagine the queues for the other two! Pooh!)

Football foul

By the second half of the 1800s work brought the Scots crowding into the big cities. But, as they say, 'All work and no play makes Jock a dull boy.' But what could these thousands of young men play?

It had to be something they could beat the English at. What better than football? It grew as the national sport of Scotland, though it had been around for hundreds of years.

- James IV's parliament had banned football back in 1491 because it was a waste of time. The game had hardly had any rules at all but it was a good excuse for a punch-up.
- In the 1500s the men of the Borders played the first 'internationals' between England and Scotland. They suffered more broken legs than a centipede under a steamroller.
- In 1568 Mary Queen of Scots watched a match at Carlisle between 20 of her followers and a team of English soldiers. An English reporter said the Scots had 'more skilful players'. What a creep.

- Sir Walter Scott enjoyed watching the holiday games in the Border towns. In Jedburgh, for example, the men of the Upper Town (called the Uppies) played the men of the Lower Town (called the Doonies) watched by the usual mob of screaming fans (probably called the Loonies).

Rangers v. Rovers

England and Scotland have a great rivalry when it comes to football. Not many people realize this goes back 400 years ... and the English cheated but the Scots slaughtered them anyway!

In 1599, six Scots of the cattle-thieving Armstrong family crossed the border to play a six-a-side against a team of English boys in Bewcastle. After the game they had a good drink in the Bewcastle Tavern before staggering home.

An Englishman called Ridley decided to capture the Scottish cattle thieves while they were on the English side of the Border. He lay in wait on the road back to Scotland.

But, somehow, the Armstrongs heard about the plot and 200 Scots rode down to the rescue and attacked Ridley's force. They killed two and captured 30 of the English cheats.

We don't know the score in the football match, but a report did describe the injuries in the fight after the match…

> Many were badly hurt, especially John Whitfield, whose bowels came out, but are sowed up again.

Banned boot boys

In the 1870s the skilled men were given Saturday afternoons off and in the 1890s the unskilled men got time off too. Football could get really big crowds now.

In 1867 the Queen's Park club was founded. Now you can't have very good matches with just one team. So they looked around for other people to play and joined the English Football Association. Scots footballers played for English clubs and Preston North End had a Scot playing for them. Strangely he brought about the end of the Scottish clubs playing in England…

March 1886   **1 penny**

The Sunday Scot

FANS FOUL FURY AT FOOTBALL

The evil English football chiefs will meet tomorrow and ban our fabulous football teams from playing in England. In yesterday's game between Queen's Park and Preston a crowd riot broke out following a fair foul on a Preston player. Pathetic Preston whinged when Queen's Park's brave back took the ball off a Preston winger.

'I won the ball fair and

square,' our skilful Scot said today. 'I hardly touched the lad's leg and it just sort of snapped in two. Of course I stumbled a bit and that's how he got those stud marks on his face. Anyway, it served him right. He'd been saying rude words to me right from the kick-off.'

Our skilful Scot

When Preston fans saw the tackle they rushed onto the pitch to batter our back and the referee called a halt to the match. The arrogant English are blaming the Queen's Park player for the riot and will try to ban Scots teams from their league. This will save them the humiliation of being beaten every week.

The Preston player was not that badly hurt. A hospital spokesman said, 'He is not quite so sick as a parrot and he should be walking without crutches in a year or two.'

Curiously enough the injured Preston player was a Scot.

Test a football fan
First find a football fan. They often paint their faces with their national flag so you can spot them easily.

Then ask them the following questions. If they get an answer correct, give them a goal; if they get it wrong give yourself a goal.

True or false…?
1 After the Preston punch-up Scottish teams were banned from playing in an English league. But English teams can play in a Scottish league.
2 In the 1880s the Scottish cup winners would play the English cup winners. The winners of that match would call themselves 'champions of Britain'.

3 The Scottish churches tried to ban football in the 1880s because it was too rough.

4 The first Association Football match between England and Scotland was played on a cricket pitch.

Answers: **1** True. Berwick Rangers (in England) play their football in Scotland ... they don't beat many Scottish teams so they are allowed to stay in the Scottish league!

2 False. Nothing as modest as that! They actually called themselves 'champions of the world'!

3 False. The churches encouraged young men to play football. A Catholic priest founded Celtic as a church youth club and in 1887 they became the famous football club.

4 True. The first Scotland v. England match was played at West of Scotland Cricket Ground in Partick in 1872. Twenty-one years later they played the international in Hampden Park in front of 102,000 people. It was the biggest stadium anywhere in the world at the time. That's how popular football was.

Bobby of the boneyard

While the Victorians made their workers slave in filthy factories for 12 hours a day, they had some strange ideas of kindness. If a beggar turned up on their doorstep they may be turned away or arrested. But let a dog do it and that was a different matter. Books have been written about Greyfriars Bobby and a film made. Of course these are sentimental Victorian slush. What you want is the true horrible history of Greyfriars Bobby. And here it is...

Greyfriars Churchyard, Edinburgh, 1858

The scruffy little Skye terrier watched as the coffin of John Gray was lowered into its grave in Greyfriars Churchyard.

As his old master disappeared below the ground, the terrier cursed. 'What a flaming nuisance! Where's me next bone coming from, that's what I want to know.' He was fed up and he looked it.

A lady in a black dress and matching veil snivelled into a handkerchief and turned away from the graveside. 'Oh, look!' she cried. The men in black suits and black top hats turned as she pointed to the Skye terrier.

'Here we go,' the terrier sighed. 'They're probably going to throw me out of the graveyard. No dogs allowed, I'll bet! Where's a terrier supposed to have a widdle if it's not against a nice cool gravestone?'

'It's little Bobby!' the woman sighed. 'It's old Jock's pet dog. Come to bid his last farewell to his master!'

'Ahhhh! Isn't he cute?' the woman next to her sighed.

'And loyal,' a man with white whiskers nodded. 'Just like old Jock himself. A trusty constable for all his life.'

'And now he's sitting there because he can't bear to leave his master!' the first woman cried.

'No, madam,' scruffy little Bobby growled. 'I'm sitting here 'cos there's nowhere else to go.'

'Would you like a bone?' the woman asked.

'Yep!' Bobby yapped.

'I'll take him up to my restaurant,' the man said. Bobby trotted at his heels and, as the man laid a plate of stewed beef and ribs on the floor, Bobby heard the gun on Edinburgh Castle fire. It did that every day at one o'clock.

Bobby trotted back to the graveyard to sniff some of the stones and see which of his mates had been around. He noticed that people came to the graveyard and stood and looked at him. 'What a loyal dog! Can't bear to leave his master,' they said and wept into their handkerchiefs.

Then the one o'clock gun would fire and remind Bobby it was dinner time. Off he'd trot to the restaurant for his daily meal. People came from miles around to see him eat. 'It puts you off a bit,' Bobby told an old greyhound one day. 'All those human people watching every mouthful and sniffing into rags.'

'Better than starving,' the greyhound said.

'True,' Bobby said. At that moment a couple of humans walked up the graveyard path, Bobby rested his head on his paws and whimpered. The woman held out a chocolate biscuit. Bobby took it gently, licked his lips and sighed. 'Never fails,' he said to the greyhound.

And so the scrounging hound lived happily for 14 more years. The most famous dog in Edinburgh. When bone-crunching Bobby finally died they put up a statue to him on an Edinburgh street.

The rich folk of Edinburgh treated the dog like a human hero – then they went back home and treated their human servants like dogs.

Herring heroines

The trouble with history is that it forgets to tell you what the ordinary people were doing in the past.

The Highlanders had been driven out of their mountain homes to make way for sheep. Many were given a little land on the coast and the only thing they could do was fish. So fishing villages sprang up.

In the 1800s and early 1900s the fishermen of Scotland were bringing much-needed money to their country. They couldn't have done it without the help of their wives. As an old Scottish saying went, *No man can be a fisherman without a wife.*

As you might expect, the women looked after the home. As Bella Jappy of Buckie said...

They did nothing. Our boys did nothing in the house. Nothing at all. The girls had to brush their clothes and all that sort of thing. And as for cleaning their shoes – oh, no, it was terrible to think that a man might have to do anything like that!

But the women did much more than that. Margaret Aitken described how the men were sent off to their boats…

The men wore long leather boots, soaked in oil, for the voyage and these boots had to be kept dry. So, when the men set sail, the women took off their shoes and stockings, tucked up their skirts and carried the men on their backs to the boats off the shore.

Imagine that! Would your mother carry your father to work?

The fishermen needed shellfish as bait. Who do you think waded through the freezing water to pick mussels and shell them? The women, of course.

Who waited for the fish to be landed so they could be gutted? The women. Gutting fish was a dangerous job, the knives were so sharp and they had to work so quickly. They bound their fingers and thumbs in rags to stop them nicking themselves. Annie Watt, aged 84, of Peterhead remembered…

Oh, me, if your hands were cut. I've got some marks that will go with me to the grave. It was the salt that did it, oh, aye, it would eat into your hands.

When a catch was landed they gutted fish from morning till night in summer...

> *A man would come round and tell you the herring would be in the yard at nine in the morning. I've seen me going home at three or four o'clock the next morning.*

And they had to work as fast as possible. If you took a break you lost time and you lost money ... but not much!

> *If you'd no speed, it was no use – you couldn't make much. The girls earned three-pence an hour (1¼ p!) for this lengthy task, carried on out of doors with no shelter.*

If they had any spare time they were expected to knit. Even underclothes were knitted.

> *I remember when mother would hang out father's woollen drawers to dry. If there was a frost then they'd stand up by themselves!*

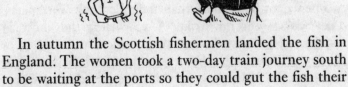

In autumn the Scottish fishermen landed the fish in England. The women took a two-day train journey south to be waiting at the ports so they could gut the fish their husbands caught.

In winter they'd cross to Ireland in boats they shared with cattle. There were no fish sheds in Ireland – they worked in the snow.

Would you have enjoyed this sort of life? Would you even survive one winter? Amazingly Annie Watt's answer, like a lot of the fish wives was...

Oh, it was fun. I wish it was those days now.

Tough ladies. Scots ladies.

The terrible 20th century

After the vicious Victorian age the 'heavy' industries started to disappear. The coal seams grew thinner and harder to work. In the 1870s miners went to America for better jobs. The ones who stayed had their wages cut.

And, also in the 1870s, the supplies of Scottish iron ore began to run out. Bad news for the shipping industry, which still needed it to build ships – and bad news for the people who worked as ship builders.

Then came the terrible 20th century. In 1914 Scots rushed to fight for Britain in the First World War ... they returned to find no one wanted their ships any more!

Did you know...?
During the First World War, American workers arrived in the engineering factories to help. They asked to be paid two pence an hour more than their Scottish workmates. The Scots went on strike. A year later the shipyard workers went on strike and their leaders were arrested. Ninety years before, rebel leaders had been beheaded or deported. In 1916 they were just deported. But where were they sent to as a punishment?

a) Australia (to work at shearing sheep and kangaroos).

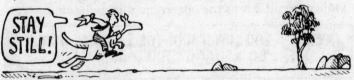

b) Germany (to fight in the war and get killed, likely as not).

c) Edinburgh.

Answer: c) What a terrible punishment for a Glasgow person! Sent to Edinburgh! (Don't worry – a lot of Edinburgh people would hate to be deported to Glasgow!)

But it wasn't long before there was a Second World War (to be fought from 1939 till 1945).

Did you know…?
In 1941 an Italian newspaper reported that the bombing of Scotland was so heavy, the Loch Ness Monster was killed by a direct hit. (The Italians said they'd made a messy of Nessie … but the newspapers were lying.)

After that war not much improved in Scotland. So, in 1949, 2,000,000 Scots signed a petition called the Scottish

Covenant asking for home rule and a Scottish assembly. They presented it to the government in London…

This upset some Scots. They blew up pillar-boxes in protest and some students pinched the stone of Scone from Westminster. The English newspapers were furious!

SAVAGE SCOTS STEAL SCONE STONE!

In the 1970s oil was discovered off the Scottish coast in the North Sea! At last, wealth for poor Scotland!

In 1979 the Scots were offered a vote on independence. A majority said 'Yes'.

BUT … the government said not enough people had voted. They refused to let Scots rule themselves.

Then, in 1997, the Labour Party won the British General Election and after a national referendum they declared that Scotland could have its own parliament.

In 2014 the Scots voted to stay in the United Kingdom. Though for some the fight for independence goes on.

Tourist terrors

Whatever happens in the future, Scotland can always enjoy looking at its bloody past. After all, that's what the tourists want to hear.

For those tourists don't just go to see the beauties of Scotland. They go to see the terrors too. If you meet one of these tourists then scare the tartan knickers off them by telling them a few truly terrible tales...

Newton Castle and Ardblair Castle, Blairgowrie

I am the ghost of Lady Jean Drummond – but you can call me Green Jean. We lived here in Newton Castle. But one day the Blairs of Ardblair Castle murdered my father and brother. The Blairs were our deadly enemies – yet I fell in love with one of them. Oh the misery! I wandered out of Newton Castle and was never seen alive again. Now, to be fair, I haunt both the castles.

Cortachy Castle, Kirriemuir

I am the phantom drummer of Cortachy. My job was to beat my drum as a warning when attackers came in sight. But the attackers paid me to stay silent. The defenders punished me by throwing me from a tower. Now I play the drum when one of the Ogilvie family is about to die. You've heard the story of me and my drum ... now beat it.

Dunphail Castle

The castle was under siege and I was one of five defenders who sneaked out to get food for the men starving inside. But we were caught, our heads were cut off and thrown over the castle wall. The attackers threw the heads and cried, 'Here's

189

beef for your bread!' We still wander the castle looking for our lost heads.

Duntrune Castle

I am the Phantom Piper of Duntrune. I entered the castle to entertain his lordship but in fact I was a spy. I warned the attackers of danger by playing my pipes. When his lordship heard this he had my hands cut off. The shock and bleeding killed me. Now I play my ghostly pipes. How do I do it when I have no hands? Because I'm a ghost, stupid![1]

Muchalls Castle

I am the Ghost of Muchalls Castle. There is a passage under the castle that leads to a cave on the seashore. My lover was a smuggler. One day I saw my lover's boat sail into the cave. I ran through the secret passage to meet him but slipped and fell in the water. By the time he landed I was drowned. Now I wander the walls, brushing my lovely hair for my lover. You couldn't lend me a hair drier, could you?

Rothesay Castle

I am the ghost of Lady Isobel and I haunt the bloody stair. My family were killed in the Viking raids and the Norse leader planned to marry me. He was horrible, so I stabbed myself to death. Sorry about the blood on the stair. Mind your feet!

1. It's said that when the castle was being repaired, there were two hands found beneath the kitchen floor!

Epilogue

In September 1997 the Scottish people voted to have their own parliament. But Scots need to look back at their horrible historical past – not the Walter Scott past – to see what they did with their freedom then.

It wasn't all cute kilts and the happiness of Highland Games in heathery hills. The history of Scotland has had some horrible moments too.

But history can be horribly interesting. Look at the way people change.

In 1883, a whale was stranded in the River Tay, near Dundee. The people of the area were thrilled. They rushed out in boats with harpoons and knives and, as the great McGonagall wrote...

> *And they laughed and grinned just like wild baboons,*
> *While they fired at him their sharp harpoons;*
> *So they got a rope from each boat tied round his tail,*
> *And landed their burden at Stonehaven without fail.*
> *So Mr John Wood has bought it for 226 pound,*
> *And brought it to Dundee all safe and sound;*
> *Which measures 40 feet in length from snout to tail,*
> *So I advise the people far and near to see it without fail.*

IS THIS GUY FOR REAL?

'FRAID SO

Many families had a great celebration at the rich supply of food and fuel the dead whales brought them.

In 1997, a whale was beached in the Firth of Forth. The people of the area were horrified. They rushed out in boats and tried to guide the creature back to the North Sea. They failed and the whale, nicknamed Moby Dick, died. Many of the watchers cried at the sad death.

People change. Life gets easier, people become kinder.

Or look at the Highland clearances.

The wealthy Duke of Sutherland was a greedy man. He had a fortune yet he wanted more. At the end of the 1790s he owned large areas of Sutherland. He and his wife found they could make more money from putting sheep on their land than from the rent of Highland crofters. So he threw the farmers and their families out of their homes to find work somewhere else or starve.

In 1998, rich owners of Scottish land can still be greedy men. They have fortunes and yet they want more. Some have discovered that they can make more money from putting grouse and deer on their land than they can from the rent of Highland farmers. So some landowners are trying to throw the farmers and their families out of their homes to find work somewhere else or starve.

Some things never change. Greedy people will always be with us. History in the past has been horrible. History in the future will go on being horrible while there are people like that around.

Still, look on the bright side. The future of Scotland has to be happier and less bloody than its horrible historical past!

INTERESTING INDEX

HORRIBLE HISTORIES

"He's a real knight-mare."

ENGLAND

Terry Deary Illustrated by Martin Brown

HORRIBLE HISTORIES

"Home is where the harp is."

IRELAND

Terry Deary Illustrated by Martin Brown

HORRIBLE HISTORIES

"I'm a minor miner."

WALES

Terry Deary Illustrated by Martin Brown

HORRIBLE HISTORIES

"Daddy was a baddy."

CRUEL KINGS AND
MEAN QUEENS

Terry Deary

HORRIBLE HISTORIES

"I hate the knight shift"

DARK KNIGHTS AND DINGY CASTLES

Terry Deary

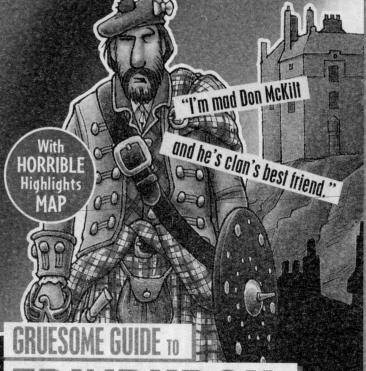

HORRIBLE HISTORIES

With **HORRIBLE** Highlights **MAP**

"I'm mad Don McKilt and he's clan's best friend."

GRUESOME GUIDE TO
EDINBURGH

Terry Deary

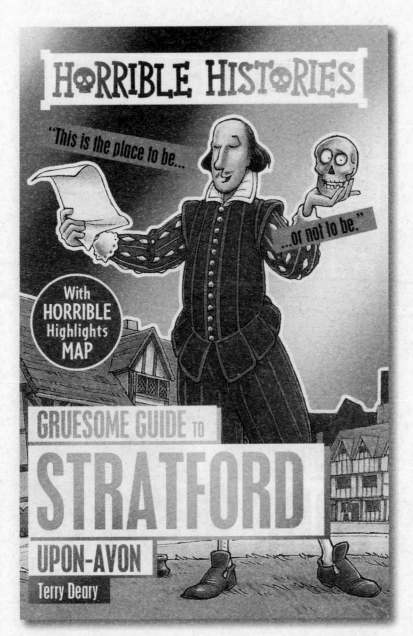

HORRIBLE HISTORIES
"I've got a degree
and he's got a pedigree."
With HORRIBLE Highlights MAP
GRUESOME GUIDE TO
OXFORD
Terry Deary Illustrated by Martin Brown

HORRIBLE HISTORIES

"Alive

alive

With **HORRIBLE** Highlights **MAP**

oh!"

GRUESOME GUIDE TO
DUBLIN

Terry Deary

HORRIBLE HISTORIES

FEATURING 50 FOUL HOUSES

"I'm the ghostess with the mostest."

GRUESOME
GREAT HOUSES

Terry Deary Illustrated by Martin Brown

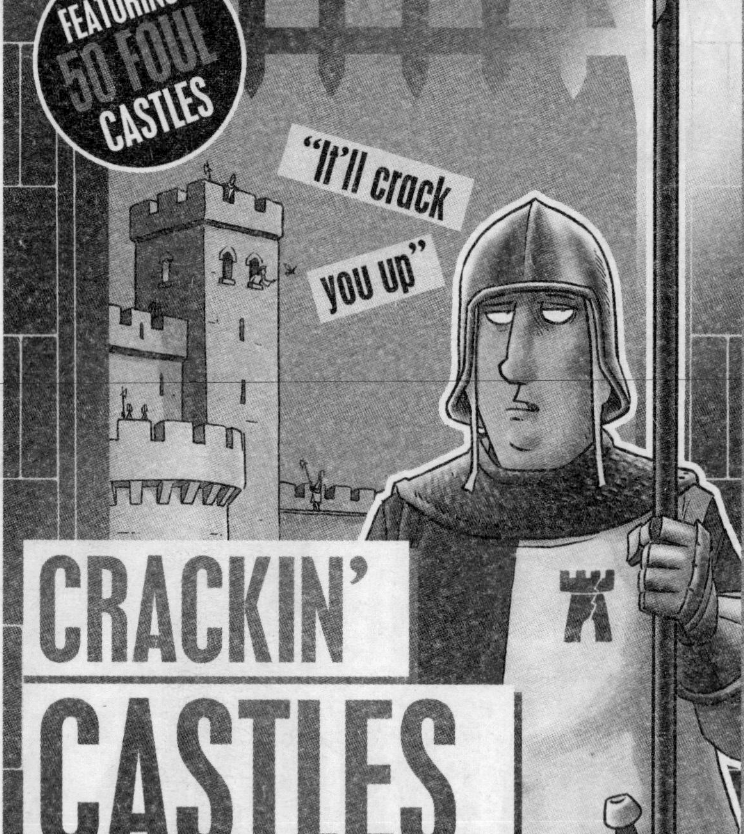
HORRIBLE HISTORIES
FEATURING 50 FOUL CASTLES
"It'll crack you up"
CRACKIN' CASTLES
Terry Deary illustrated by Martin Brown